# 話すための英語
### ニュース・ビジネス&スポーツ編(上)

井上一馬
*Inoue Kazuma*

PHP新書

## はじめに

　この本は、『話すための英語 日常会話編（上・下）』の姉妹編です。

　「日常会話編」では、「英語を話せるようになりたい」「日常会話ていどは話したい」と思いながら、なかなか話せるようにならない人のために、日常的に使われる単語、熟語、表現を、さまざまな場面ごとに学んでいきました。

　今度の「ニュース・ビジネス＆スポーツ編（略称ＮＢＳ編）」では、ニュース、ビジネス、スポーツ（主に野球とゴルフ）で使う言葉を、それぞれの分野別に勉強していきたいと思います。

　テレビのワイドショーなどを見てもわかるとおり、日常使う言葉と、硬軟とりまぜたさまざまなニュースで使われる言葉は、非常に密接な関係にあります。区別しがたいものがたくさんあります。ニュース、ビジネス、スポーツの英語は、日常会話の延長線上にあるからです。ニュース番組にも必ず、一般のニュース、ビジネスニュース、スポーツニュースが登場します。

　ですから、『話すための英語』の「日常会話編」を終えた方は、ぜひこちらの「ニュース・ビジネス＆スポーツ編」にもトライしてみてほしいと思います。**英語を話せるようになりたい人**はもちろん、**大学受験、英検、TOEIC、TOEFL** などの試験で高得点を取りたい方は、ぜひ両方勉強することをお勧めします。

　また、こちらの本を勉強する方は、ぜひその前に「日常会話編」を勉強してほしいと思います。やはり、まずは基本から入っていってほしいからです。「日常会話編」と本編には重複して登場する単語もいくつかあります

が，それぞれの場面や分野の中でその使い方を覚えていけば，より確実に英語を使いこなす力が身につくと思います。

「日常会話編」の「はじめに」の部分で書いたように，私は日本人の英語学習を，**「読むための英語」**から**「話すための英語」**へ，英語を読むための受け身の勉強から，**話すためのアクティブな勉強**へと変えていきたいと思っています。そのために，「日常会話編」に収録したすべての言葉は，これまでの多くの教材のように「英語→日本語」の順ではなく，**「日本語→英語」**の順で覚えられるようにしました。そのほうが，私たち日本語を話す日本人にとってははるかに覚えやすいからです。記憶に残りやすいからです。

また，実践に即して英語を覚えられるように，単語，熟語，表現別の分類や，品詞別の分類を撤廃し，それらをすべて一緒にして場面ごとに，関連づけて覚えられるようにしました。実際に使うときには，単語も熟語も表現も，名詞も形容詞も動詞も，一緒に使うのであって，それぞれを別々に分けて使うわけではないからです。

さらに，前置詞や動詞の使い方を覚えてもらうため，「結婚する」なら単にmarryではなく，marry him, get married to himというふうに，目的語や後にくる前置詞まで入れました。

当然のことですが，姉妹編であるこの本でも，以上の考え方にのっとって同じスタイルで言葉を収録してあります。そしてニュース，ビジネス，スポーツの英語が，「景気」「金融」「貿易摩擦」「株」「政治」「犯罪」「戦争」「国際関係」「ゴルフ」などの**分野別**にわかりやすく配置され，覚えやすくなっています。

これからはますます，日本文化を世界に向けて発信し

はじめに

ていく**発信型**のコミュニケーションが必要とされる時代になっていきます。そこでこの本では，外国人に日本のことを伝えるための言葉も多く入れました。

あなたは次にあげる日本語を英語でいえるでしょうか。

①バブル経済　②日銀短観　③カンフル剤
④波及効果　⑤住宅投資　⑥景気をテコ入れする
⑦貸し渋り　⑧公的資金　⑨含み益
⑩粉飾決算　⑪労務管理　⑫資本提携
⑬産業の空洞化　⑭協調介入に踏み切る　⑮投資家
⑯税制優遇措置　⑰統一地方選　⑱国民投票
⑲選挙違反　⑳小選挙区比例代表並立制
㉑格差を2倍以内に抑える　㉒日和見を決め込む
㉓五十歩百歩だ　㉔少子化　㉕単身赴任
㉖介護保険　㉗オゾン層の破壊　㉘酸性雨
㉙環境にやさしい　㉚汚染源　㉛脳死判定をする
㉜拒絶反応　㉝体外受精　㉞合同軍事演習
㉟後方支援　㊱ガイドライン法案　㊲最多勝投手
㊳牽制球を投げる　㊴黒星を喫する　㊵パーをとる

もしうまく英語にできなかったら，ぜひこの本で勉強してみてください。きっとイモづる式にどんどん覚えていけるはずです。

とはいえ，外国語を学ぶのはやはり根気のいる大変な作業です。外国人が長いあいだかかって自然に覚えるものを，一気に人工的に覚えようというのですから。

また日常会話でもそうですが，コミュニケーションというのは相手の話を聞いてわからなければ成立しないので，ニュース英語でもかなりの数の単語，熟語，表現を

覚える必要が出てきます。
　したがってこの本でも、「日常会話編」と同じように、分野別に少しずつ，勉強していきたいと思います。
　それではそろそろニュース・ビジネス＆スポーツの英語の勉強を始めましょう。

# *contents*

はじめに 3
この本の見方, 使い方 12

## *part* 1 景気・バブル・不況

好景気 14
不況対策 16
インフレ 20
不況 15
消費, 投資 18

## *part* 2 金　融

金融システム 22
融資 24
銀行救済 27
金融破綻 30
銀行 23
不良債権, 債権 25
監査 29

## *part* 3 合理化・合併

リストラ 34
年金 37
合併, 提携, 買収 39
労使関係 35
経費節減 38
慈善活動 41

## part 4 貿易摩擦

自由貿易, 保護貿易 44
貿易摩擦 46
日米経済摩擦 49
日本の企業社会 51

収支 45
市場開放 48
談合 50

## part 5 為替相場

為替市場 54
通貨政策 55

円相場 54

## part 6 株・株式市場

株 58
値上がり 62
市場の様子 65

株価 61
値下がり 64
債券, 金融商品 67

## part 7 税 金

税金 70
税制改革 72

課税, 免税 71

## part 8 相撲 〈ちょっとひと休み〉

力士, 場所 76
勝敗 80
取組 78

## part 9 選挙

選挙 84
日本の選挙 85
選挙運動 88
投票 91
アメリカの選挙 84
立候補, 候補者 87
世論調査 90
選挙結果 92

## part 10 政治・政党

政体 96
アメリカの政体 99
保守, 革新 103
自民党 105
長老 108
主義 98
日本の政体 101
政党 104
派閥 106

## part 11 権力闘争

主導権 112
傍観 115
危機 117
論争 119
根回し 112
一匹狼 116
逆転, 変革 118
中傷合戦 121

## part 12 国会・法案

三権分立 126  
議会 127  
法案 129  
混乱, 紛糾 134  
国会 126  
アメリカの議会 128  
予算 132  
法律 135  

## part 13 官僚・行政改革

議員活動 140  
官僚, 行政改革 144  
コラム——省庁の名前 146  
不正, 賄賂 140  
地方分権 145  

## part 14 ニュービジネス・ニューテクノロジー

先端技術 150  
コンピュータ 151  
特許, 知的所有権 151  
ニュービジネス 154  

## part 15 社会・文化

少子化問題 158  
高齢化社会 159  
オウム 162  
映画 164  
家族の問題 159  
若者の風俗, 問題 160  
サッカー人気 163  
叙勲, 文化遺産 165

## part 16 野　球

球場　168
勝負, 順位　169
勝利投手, 敗戦投手　175
三振　177
フォアボール　180
打者, 打撃　183
さまざまな打球　187
長打　190
打点　192
守備　195
練習　198

シーズン　168
投手陣　174
投球　176
コース, カウント　178
死球, 調子　181
打席に入って　185
ヒット　189
ホームラン　191
走塁　193
エラー　198

コラム ── 選手・監督　172

日本語索引　200
英語索引　222

---
**下巻の内容**

環境問題　　宇宙　　生命・医療
差別問題　　犯罪　　警察・捜査
裁判・刑罰　　軍隊・兵器　　戦争
内戦・反政府運動　　国際関係・国連・安保
交渉・条約　　ゴルフ

# この本の見方, 使い方

| | |
|---|---|
| ◆**銀行** | |
| 金融機関 | financial institution<br>金融商品 financial instrument |
| 国際決済銀行 | Bank of International Settlement ❶<br>[BIS] |
| 日銀[日本銀行] | ① Bank of Japan ② central bank ❷<br>日銀総裁　governor<br>銀行の「頭取」のことは president といいます。 |
| ノンバンク | non-bank（financial institution）❸ |
| 信用金庫 | credit assocíation ❹<br>信用組合 credit union【júːnjən】❺ |
| 支店長 | branch manager |
| モフ担 | person [company official] in charge ❶<br>of the Ministry of Finance<br>モフは Ministry of Finance（大蔵省）の頭文字 MOF からきています。 |

❶ 英語の熟語や表現の中で, 別の言葉でいいかえられる場合には, [　] で別の言葉を補ってあります。上の例の場合, Bank of International Settlement を BIS ともいうことができます。また, person in charge of the ～ を company official in charge of the ～ といいかえてもいいわけです。

❷ 1つの日本語に対して2つ以上の英語がある場合には, ①, ②と並べて覚えられるようにしてあります。

❸ 英語の熟語や表現の中で省略してもよい言葉については, その言葉を（　）でくくってあります。ただし, merge（with）のような場合は, うしろに目的語がくるときにとる前置詞を表します。

❹ assocíation の ´ マークはアクセント記号です。特に注意を要する単語のみに付してあります。

❺ 発音記号は, 特に発音しにくいと思われる単語のみに付し, 注意を要するものにはカタカナ読みを記してあります。発音はアメリカ英語を基本としました。

# part 1

# 景気・バブル・不況

①好景気
②景気がよくなる
③バブル経済
④日銀短観
⑤市場は飽和状態だ
⑥カンフル剤
⑦即効
⑧波及効果
⑨内需拡大
⑩住宅投資
これをあなたは英語でいえますか？

# ◆好景気

| | |
|---|---|
| 景気 | ① economy 【ikánəmi】<br>② económic [business] conditions |
| 好況 | ① good business conditions<br>② humming economy |
| 活発な, 活気に満ちた | ① vibrant ② vital ③ robúst<br>robust になると「強靱な, 力強い」という意味合いが出てきます。vital には「非常に重要な」という意味もあります。 |
| 好景気(になる) | boom<br>景気がよくなる。<br>The economy is booming. |
| バブル経済 | ① bubble economy<br>② economic bubble<br>バブル経済の崩壊<br>① collapse of the bubble economy<br>② bursting of the bubble economy<br>burst は「破裂する」という意味です。 |
| 経済が加熱しすぎる危険がある。 | The economy could overheat.<br>この could は仮定法の could です。 |
| 景気動向指数 | diffusion index [DI] |
| 豊かさ指標, 新国民生活指標 | people's life indicators |
| 日銀短観[企業短期経済観測調査] | the Bank of Japan's quarterly survey<br>経済白書 economic white paper |
| 景気循環 | business cycle |

part 1 ● 景気・バブル・不況

# ◆不況

| | |
|---|---|
| 不況, 不景気 | depression |
| 景気後退 | recession<br>構造不況 structural recession |
| 景気停滞 | stagnation<br>停滞した, よどんだ stagnant |
| 景気低迷 | ① slump<br>スポーツ選手の「スランプ」と同じです。<br>② doldrums<br>複数で使います。 |
| 未然に防ぐ | forestall |
| 長びく不況 | ① ailing economy<br>② lingering recession |
| 輝きのない年 | lackluster year |
| 経済危機 | economic crisis<br>経済的混乱 economic chaos 【kéiɑs】 |
| 低迷する自動車販売 | sluggish auto sales<br>sluggishの他, 上のstagnantやslowなども使えます。 |
| 市場は飽和状態だ。 | **The market has been saturated.**<br>市場は横ばいが続いている。<br>**The market has been flat.**<br>もちろん, The sales have been flat.「売り上げは横ばいが続いている」という言い方もできます。 |

| | |
|---|---|
| 収益が伸び悩む。 | The earnings continue to lag.<br>lag は「遅れをとる，ぐずぐずする」という意味です。<br>アフリカ系アメリカ人は経済面で白人に遅れをとっている。<br>African-Americans still lag behind whites financially. |
| 結果として生じる | ① result（from） ② stem（from）<br>この不景気は政府の誤った経済政策の結果として生じている。<br>This recession results from the wrong economic policies of the government. |
| 根本的原因 | root cause |

## ◆不況対策

| | |
|---|---|
| 金融緩和策 | easy-money policy<br>金融引締策 tight-money policy<br>単に「引締策，緊縮策」というときは，belt-tightening policy ともいいます。<br>「引き締める」は tighten です。 |
| 強化する | ① reinforce ② intensify |
| このままでいく，現状を維持する | stand［stay］put |
| 公定歩合 | official discount rate |
| 財政出動 | fiscal［financial］action |

## part 1 ● 景気・バブル・不況

| | |
|---|---|
| | 行動する take action |
| 景気を刺激する，テコ入れする | ① stimulate the economy<br>② boost the economy |
| 景気対策を講ずる | take measures to stimulate the economy |
| 遅くとも3月までに | by March at the latest<br>早くとも at the earliest |
| 景気上昇 | upturn of the economy<br>景気回復 economic recovery |
| 景気が回復しつつある。 | The economy is recovering.<br>2年8カ月ぶりに新車の販売が上昇した。<br>Sales of new cars were up first for two years and eight months. |
| マイナスに働く | hamper efforts<br>hamper は「妨げる」という意味です。 |
| カンフル剤 | a shot in the arm |
| 即効 | immediate effect<br>相乗効果 synergy |
| 波及効果 | ripple effect<br>波及効果をもたらす<br>make a ripple effect |
| 経済成長 | economic growth<br>プラス成長 positive growth<br>マイナス成長 negative growth<br>ゼロ成長 zero growth |
| 3％の経済成長を維持する | maintain 3% economic growth |

| | |
|---|---|
| 持続可能な成長 | sustainable growth<br>sustain は「支える」という意味です。<br>下支えする bolster |
| 内需 | domestic demand<br>⇔外需 external demand |
| 内需拡大 | expansion of the domestic demand |
| 需要 | demand<br>個人需要 consumer demand |
| 供給 | supply<br>供給過剰 oversupply |
| 国内総生産 | gross domestic product ［GDP］ |
| 国民総生産 | gross national product ［GNP］ |

## ◆消費, 投資

| | |
|---|---|
| 消費者物価 | consumer prices<br>複数で使います。<br>卸売物価 wholesale prices<br>小売り価格, 物価 retail prices |
| 基準価格 | benchmark price<br>価格をつり上げる jack up the price |
| 個人消費 | ① personal consumption<br>② personal spending |
| 個人消費の落ち込み | decline of the personal consumption<br>回復 recovery |

*part 1* ● 景気・バブル・不況

| | |
|---|---|
| 惜し気ない消費 | lavish spending |
| エンゲル係数 | Engel's coefficient |
| 消費者が元気を取り戻しつつある。 | Consumers are perking up.<br>perk up はまさに「元気になる，元気を取り戻す」という意味です。 |
| 大量生産 | mass production<br>**量産する** churn out<br>churn は本来「(クリーム，ミルクなどを)かきまぜる」の意味です。 |
| 大量消費 | mass consumption |
| 公共投資 | public investment<br>**公共事業** public works |
| 民間投資 | private sector investment |
| 設備投資 | ① investment in plant and equipment<br>② plant and equipment investment<br>③ capital investment |
| 設備過剰,過剰設備 | ① overcapacity ② excess capacity |
| インフラの整備 | improvement of infrastructure<br>英語では infra と略さないことに注意してください。 |
| 住宅投資 | housing starts<br>これは正確には，「住宅建設着工(数)」のことです。 |
| 持ち家率 | home ownership rate<br>**マイカー普及率** car ownership rate |
| 公団 | public corporation |

| | |
|---|---|
| 行政指導 | administrative guidance<br>administrative は「行政の」という意味で,「行政」は administration です。 |
| 国営企業 | ① state-run company<br>② state-owned company<br>民間企業 private company |
| 民営化 | privatizátion<br>民営化する prívatize |
| 多国籍企業 | multinational company<br>世界を股にかける企業<br>globe-trotting company |
| 巨大企業 | juggernaut【dʒʌ́gərnɔ̀ːt】<br>無敵の invíncible |

# ◆インフレ

| | |
|---|---|
| 二桁のインフレ | two-digit inflation<br>デフレ deflation<br>景気低迷下のインフレ stagflation |
| インフレ対策 | anti-inflation policy<br>「対策」には measures（通例, 複数）も使えます。<br>インフレ緩和 disinflation |
| インフレと闘う | fight inflation |
| インフレを抑制する | ① keep a grip on inflation<br>② curtail inflation |

# part 2

# 金　融

①金融改革
②日銀総裁
③ゼネコン
④不良債権の開示基準
⑤貸し渋り
⑥公的資金
⑦含み益
⑧粉飾決算
⑨社会的信用を失う
⑩破綻する
これをあなたは英語でいえますか？

# ◆ 金融システム

| | |
|---|---|
| 金融システム | financial system<br>金融システムの安定<br>**stability of the financial system**<br>「〜を目指す」なら aim at,「〜を実現する」なら realize が使えます。 |
| 安定化する | stabilize【stéibəlàiz】<br>安定化 stabilizátion<br>金融システムをかろうじて安定化させる<br>**manage to stabilize the financial system** |
| 金融業界 | financial industry<br>銀行業界 banking industry |
| 金融自由化 | financial liberalization |
| 日銀と大蔵省は金融自由化をめぐって対立している。 | **The Bank of Japan and the Finance Ministry are at odds over financial liberalization.**<br>be at odds は「対立している」というときにニュース英語でよく使う表現なのでしっかり覚えておいてください。<br>各省庁の名前については、後のコラムに出てきます。 |
| 金融改革 | financial reforms<br>ふつう複数で使います。<br><br>金融改革の速度を早める<br>**speed financial reforms** |

*part 2* ● 金融

| | |
|---|---|
| | 「早める」には **precipitate** という言葉も使えます。precipitate には，形容詞で「まっしぐらの，まっ逆さまの」という意味もあり，**precipitation** は「促進，急落」などの意味になります。 |
| 促進する | **accelerate**【æksélərèit】<br>促進 **acceleration**<br>物理では「加速度」の意味もあります。車のアクセルは accelerator といいます。「日常会話編」でやりましたね。 |

## ◆ 銀行

| | |
|---|---|
| 金融機関 | **financial institution**<br>金融商品 **financial instrument** |
| 国際決済銀行 | **Bank of International Settlement [BIS]** |
| 日銀[日本銀行] | ① **Bank of Japan** ② **central bank**<br>日銀総裁 **governor**<br>銀行の「頭取」のことは **president** といいます。 |
| 都市銀行 | **city bank**<br>地方銀行 **regional bank** |
| 信託銀行 | **trust bank** |
| 長期信用銀行 | **long-term credit bank** |
| ノンバンク | **non-bank（financial institution）** |

| | |
|---|---|
| 信用金庫 | credit association<br>信用組合 credit union 【júːnjən】 |
| 支店長 | branch manager |
| モフ担 | person [company official] in charge of the Ministry of Finance<br>モフは Ministry of Finance (大蔵省) の頭文字 MOF からきています。 |
| 損保［損害保険会社］ | casualty insurance company<br>生保［生命保険会社］<br>life insurance company |
| 銀行の利益は今後も増え続ける見通しだ。 | Banks' profits are likely to continue increasing.<br>お金をすくい取る skim money |

## ◆融資

| | |
|---|---|
| 融資する,貸し付ける | ① lend ② finance |
| 融資,貸し付け | ① loan ② lending ③ financing |
| 融資基準 | lending guidelines |
| 融資限度枠 | limit on the amount of loans<br>融資限度枠を設定する<br>set a limit on the amount of loans<br>越える ① go over ② exceed |
| 過剰融資 | excessive loan [lending]<br>不正融資 illegal loan [lending] |

| | |
|---|---|
| 担保 | **colláteral**<br>collateral には条約などの「付帯事項」の意味もあります。<br>抵当 mortgage【mɔ́ːrgidʒ】 |
| 保証人 | **voucher**【váutʃər】 |
| 不動産 | **real estate**<br>不動産業者 realtor【ríːəltər】 |
| 不動産開発業者 | **developer**<br>地上げ屋 land shark |
| ゼネコン | **general contractor** |
| 地価 | **land price**<br>地価の下落 decline of land prices |
| 地価が落ちついてくる。 | **Land prices are leveling off.** |
| 所有者 | ① **owner** ② **propríetor** |
| 遊休地 | **idled land**<br>空地 clearing |
| (地域の)高級化 | **gentrification**<br>高級化する gentrify |
| (都市などの)改造 | **facelift**<br>「美容整形」の意味もあります。 |

## ◆ 不良債権, 債権

| | |
|---|---|
| 不良債権 | ① **bad loan [debt]**<br>② **nonperforming loan** |

| | |
|---|---|
| 回収可能な | collectible<br>回収不能な uncollectible |
| 回収する | retrieve |
| 遅延の | overdue |
| 不良債権を管理する,追跡する | keep track of bad loans |
| 不良債権の開示基準 | disclosure standards of bad loans |
| 情報開示,情報公開 | disclosure<br>情報を開示する,公開する<br>disclose the information |
| 透明性 | transparency |
| 健全性 | soundness<br>健全な ① sound ② wholesome |
| 帳消しにする | write off<br>負担する shoulder |
| 段階的に整理する,除去する | phase out<br>phase は名詞では「局面」の意味です。 |
| 相殺する | offsét<br>債務を債権で相殺する<br>offset debts against credits |
| 債務,負債,借金 | debt【det】<br>債権 credit |
| 債務者,借り方 | debtor<br>債権者,貸し方 creditor |
| 債務返済能力 | debt-serving capability |

| | |
|---|---|
| 債務不履行 | **default**<br>スポーツの「不戦勝」のことは win by default といいます。 |
| 送金(手段) | **remíttance**<br>送金する remit |
| 充当する, 当てる | ① **állocate** ② **appropriate** |

## ◆銀行救済

| | |
|---|---|
| 格付け会社 | **credit-rating agency** |
| 自己資本比率 | **capital ádequacy requirement**<br>自己資本 equity【ékwəti】 |
| 運転資金 | **operating funds**<br>流動資産 liquid assets |
| 貸し渋り | **credit crunch**<br>crunch は「危機」とか「ピンチ」の意味です。「金融逼迫(ひっぱく)」は financial crunch といいます。 |
| 銀行が貸し渋る。 | **Banks are reluctant to lend money.** |
| 先細りになる | **taper off** |
| 公的資金 | **public fund [money]** |
| 注入する | **inject**<br>注入 injection<br>「注射(する)」と同じ言葉を使います。 |
| 受け入れ行 | **recipient**【risípiənt】 |

| | |
|---|---|
| | recipient は receive する人のことで、「保険受給者」や「移植を受ける人」などのことも意味します。 |
| 法的根拠 | **legal identity**<br>法的根拠を付する<br>attach legal identity（to） |
| 経常利益 | **pretax profits**<br>⇔ 経常赤字 pretax losses |
| 純益 | ① **net（business）profit**<br>② **net earnings** |
| 増益 | **increase in profits**<br>⇔ 減益 fall［reduction］in profits |
| 仕入れ原価 | **costs of purchase** |
| 含み益 | **hidden profit**<br>⇔ 含み損 hidden loss<br>留保利益 retained earnings |
| 最終利益 | **bottom line**<br>帳簿のいちばん下の行（bottom line）に表示されることからこの言葉が生まれました。ニュース英語ではこの言葉を「問題の要点」の意味でもよく使います。 |
| 損益分岐点 | **break-even point**<br>収支が合う break even |
| 未払い残高 | **outstanding balance**<br>outstanding には「目立つ、顕著な」の意味の他に、「未払いの、未解決の」の意味があります。 |

| | |
|---|---|
| 最優遇貸出金利 | prime rate |
| 劣後ローン | subordinated loan |
| 逆ざや | back spread |
| もうけもの, たなぼた, 意外な授かり物 | windfall<br>もともとは「風で落ちた果物」などのことでした。 |
| 損益計算書 | ① profit and loss statement [P/L]<br>② income statement |
| 年2回の | biannual |
| 一年につき | per annum<br>一人につき, 一人当たり per capita<br>一日につき per diem<br>これは正式な言い方で, 日常会話ではそれぞれ per year, per person, per day ということができます。 |

## ◆監査

| | |
|---|---|
| 監査する, 検査する | inspect<br>監査, 検査 inspection |
| 決算 | book-closing<br>連結決算 consólidated book-closing [statements]<br>consolidate は「まとめる」の意味です。 |
| 粉飾(決算) | window dressing (financial records) |
| 帳簿をごまかす | falsify the book(s) |

| | |
|---|---|
| | 帳簿を照合する<br>reconcile the book(s) |
| 是正措置 | corrective action<br>是正措置を強く求める<br>press the bank for corrective action |
| 帳簿外の | off-the-book |
| トンネル会社 | dummy company<br>架空会社 fictitious company |
| 背任 | breach of trust<br>breach は「違反，不履行」の意味で，breach of promise といえば「約束違反」, breach of the peace といえば「治安妨害」の意味になります。 |
| 社会的信用を失う | ① lose public confidence<br>② suffer from the loss of public confidence |
| 社会的信用を回復する | regain battered public confidence<br>batter は「台無しにする」という意味です。 |
| 職業倫理 | professional ethics |

## ◆金融破綻

| | |
|---|---|
| 破綻する | fail<br>破綻した日本債権信用銀行<br>failed Nippon Credit Bank |

## part 2 ● 金融

| | |
|---|---|
| | **破綻 failure**<br>「破綻(する)」はもちろん「倒産(する)」と置きかえることも可能です。 |
| 倒産 | **bankruptcy**【bǽŋkrʌptsi】<br>bankruptcyには「破産」の意味もあります。 |
| 倒産する | ① go out of business<br>② go bankrupt ③ bust<br>④ go bust ⑤ go under |
| 倒産は避けられない。 | Bankruptcy is inevitable. |
| 暗礁に乗り上げる | go on the rocks |
| 破綻せずにいる | stay afloat |
| 今はなき, 消滅した | now defúnct |
| 試練 | ordéal<br>**厳しい試練を受ける run the gauntlet**<br>gauntletは, 2列に並んだ人間がそのあいだを通る罪人をむちで打つ刑のことです。 |
| 困難 | hardship |
| 会社更生法 | **Corporate Reorganization Law**<br>会社更生手続きを申請する<br>file for bankruptcy protection |
| 管財人 | receiver |
| 預金保険機構 | ① deposit-insurance system for banks<br>② deposit-insurance corporation |

| | |
|---|---|
| 預金はすべて保護されます。 | All the deposits are guaranteed. |
| 清算する | liquidate 【líkwidèit】<br>清算 liquidation |
| 受け皿銀行 | bridge bank<br>つなぎ融資 emergency loan |
| 整理回収銀行 | resolution and collection bank |
| 救済措置 | bail(-)out<br>救済する bail out |
| 救済計画 | rescue scheme [plan]<br>再建策,再建計画 restructure plan |
| 債務超過 | excess of debts over assets<br>超過する ① exceed ② surpass |
| 手形 | ① draft ② bill<br>小切手 check |
| 裏書きする | endorse<br>裏書き人 endorser<br>裏書き endorsement |
| 不渡手形 | dishonored bill<br>この手形は不渡りです。<br>This draft is dishonored. |
| 約束手形 | prómissory note |

# part 3

# 合理化・合併

①リストラ
②余剰人員
③史上最悪の失業率
④求人倍率
⑤労働争議
⑥労務管理
⑦労働基準法
⑧資本提携
⑨詳細は明らかにされなかった
⑩分社化する
これをあなたは英語でいえますか？

# ◆ リストラ

| | |
|---|---|
| リストラ | restructuring<br>リストラの対象になる<br>become a target of restructuring |
| 大胆な | drastic |
| 余剰人員 | surplus in labor force |
| 余分な | redúndant<br>**余剰労働者** redundant workers<br>redundant には「冗漫な,冗長な」という意味もあり，redundant sentence といえば,「冗漫な文章」のことです。<br>**余分,冗漫さ** redundancy |
| 人員過剰問題 | overstaffing problem |
| 人員削減 | cutback(s) in personnel [staff] |
| 新規補充をしない人員削減 | cutbacks by attrition<br>attrition は「摩耗,自然消耗」のことです。 |
| 雇用者数を少なめに申告する | understate its employment<br>その場しのぎの数字を並べる<br>fudge the figures |
| 解雇する,免職にする | ① dismiss ② discharge<br>**解雇,免職** ① dismissal ② discharge<br>このあたりのことに関しては,「日常会話編」の仕事の章も参照してください。<br>**〜を理由に** on (the) grounds of |

| | |
|---|---|
| 解雇通知 | walking papers |
| 懲戒(する) | réprimand |
| 懲戒免職 | disciplinary dismissal<br>懲戒処分 disciplinary action |
| 史上最悪の失業率 | record high unemployment ［jobless］rate<br>「(史上最悪の失業率を) 記録する」といいたいときには mark を使います。 |
| 失業の可能性 | possible loss of jobs |
| 求人倍率 | ratio of job offers to job-seekers |
| 離職(率) | turnover (rate) |

## ◆労使関係

| | |
|---|---|
| 労使関係 | management-labor relations |
| 労使紛争 | management-labor dispute<br>労働争議 labor dispute |
| 労働組合 | labor union<br>団結, 連帯 solidárity |
| 春闘 | spring labor offensive<br>offensive はふつう形容詞で「腹立たしい, 攻撃的な」の意味ですが, ここでは「攻勢, 攻撃」といった感じの意味になります。 |
| 団体交渉 | collective bargaining |

| | |
|---|---|
| | 駆引の材料 bargaining chip<br>駆引をする bargain (over) |
| ピケ隊, ピケを張る | picket |
| 賃上げ要求 | wage claim<br>賃金凍結 wage freeze |
| 単純平均, 数字上の平均 | aríthmetic average<br>arithmeticは「算数」という意味ですから、「単なる計算上の平均」ということになります。 |
| ILO[国際労働機関] | International Labor Organization [ILO] |
| 労働基準法 | Labor Standards Law<br>労働基準法で労働時間は週40時間と定められている。<br>The Labor Standards Law sets working hours at 40 hours per week. |
| 労務管理 | labor management<br>労災 labor accident |
| 男女雇用機会均等法 | Equal Employment Opportunity Law |
| 同一労働同一賃金 | equal pay for equal work |
| セクハラ | sexual harassment<br>セクハラを受けたことがありますか？<br>Have you (ever) suffered sexual harassment? |

## ◆年金

| | |
|---|---|
| 企業年金 | corporate pension [annuity]<br>企業年金制度は見直される。<br>**The corporate pension system will be reviewed.** |
| 厚生年金 | employees' pension<br>国民年金 national pension |
| 老齢年金 | old-age pension<br>遺族年金 ① survivor's pension<br>② survivorship |
| 年金基金 | pension funds |
| 積立金 | contribution |
| (年金の)支払い | payout |
| 確定給付契約 | guaranteed investment contract |
| 日本版401ｋプラン<br>[確定拠出型年金] | Japanese version of the 401(k) plan<br>アメリカの内国歳入法（Internal Revenue Code）の401条(k)項の規定からこう呼ばれています。 |
| 401(k)プランを<br>軽視する, 加入を<br>見合わせる | forgo 401k plans |
| メディケイド | Medicaid<br>メディケア Medicare<br>メディケイドはアメリカの低所得者・障害者のための医療補助制度, メディケアは高齢者のための医療補助制度です。 |

# ◆経費節減

| | |
|---|---|
| 経費 | ① costs ② expenses<br>ふつう複数で使います。同じ経費でも, もともとの動詞の意味から, 人件費のように「かかる」感じのするものは cost, 交通費のように支払う感じのものについては, expense を多く使います。 |
| 固定費 | fixed costs<br>人件費 personnel [labor] costs |
| 必要経費 | necessary expenses |
| 交通費 | travel [transportation] expenses |
| 交際費 | (social and) entertainment expenses<br>食費 food expenses<br>医療費 medical expenses |
| 経費削減 | ① cost reduction ② cost cut |
| 経費を削減する | ① cut costs [expenses]<br>② cut back on costs<br>③ slash costs |
| 経費を抑える | curb [hold down] costs |
| 経費を節約する | save on expenses<br>これは save (money) on expenses ということです。 |
| 何らかの形で | in one way or another<br>とにかく, いずれにしても<br>in any event [case] |

| | |
|---|---|
| 合理化する | ① streamline ② rationalize<br>合理化 ① streamlining ② rationalization |
| 給与以外の福利厚生 | perks<br>perquisite の一般的な言い方で，しばしば複数で使います。 |
| 大改革 | shake-up |
| 外注 | outsourcing<br>外注する outsource |
| 工場を閉鎖する | close [shut down] a factory |
| 在庫を減らす | hold down inventories [stocks] |

## ◆合併, 提携, 買収

| | |
|---|---|
| 提携 | ① tie-up ② partnership<br>提携する tie up |
| 資本提携 | capital tie-up (with)<br>広範囲の提携<br>wide-ranging partnership |
| 詳細は明らかにされなかった。 | No details were revealed. |
| 合弁事業 | joint venture<br>合弁企業, 共同体 consórtium<br>consortium には,「開発途上国に対する国際借款団」の意味もあります。 |
| 合併 | merger |

| | |
|---|---|
| | 合併する merge（with）<br>大型合併 megamerger |
| 合併・買収（M&A） | merger and acquisition ［M&A］ |
| 吸収する | absorb<br>吸収（合併） absorption |
| 乗っ取り，買収 | takeover<br>乗っ取る take over |
| 買収する | buy<br>AOLがタイムワーナーを買収した。<br>**AOL bought Time Warner.**<br>その逆 the other way around |
| 株式公開買付 | takeover bid ［TOB］ |
| 買収の総額については口を濁した。 | He quibbled about the total amount of the takeover.<br>quibble は動詞では「はぐらかす」，名詞では「はぐらかし」の意味になります。「言葉を濁す」には **hedge** という動詞も使えます。これは名詞では「生け垣」の意味です。 |
| 分社化する | spin off<br>分社，スピンオフ spin-off |
| 持ち主が変わる | change hands |
| 規定，条件 | stipulation<br>規定する stipulate |
| 契約不履行 | breach of contract<br>破る，違反する breach |

| | |
|---|---|
| 不可抗力 | **inevitabílity**<br>法律用語では，force majeure といいます。 |

## ◆慈善活動

| | |
|---|---|
| 企業のイメージアップをする | **improve the corporate image** |
| 企業の慈善活動 | **philanthropy**【filǽnθrəpi】<br>ふつうの慈善活動は **charity**【tʃǽrəti】ですね。 |
| 慈善活動は社風に合わない。 | **Philanthropy goes against the grain.**<br>借金は私の性に合わない。<br>**Borrowing money goes against the grain.**<br>grain は「穀物」「木目, 石目」などの意味で，go against the grain で「性分に合わない」の意味になります。「目」に反するというわけです。 |
| ボランティア活動 | **volunteer activities**<br>ボランティア活動をする<br>**take part in volunteer activities** |

# part 4

# 貿易摩擦

①貿易不均衡
②拡大する貿易黒字
③前年同月比
④例外なき関税化
⑤規制緩和
⑥輸入制限
⑦産業の空洞化
⑧談合
⑨財界
⑩日経連
これをあなたは英語でいえますか？

## ◆自由貿易, 保護貿易

| | |
|---|---|
| 自由貿易 | ① free trade  ② open trade<br>自由奔放な freewheeling |
| 自由貿易体制への道を開く | pave the way for the free trade system |
| 自由放任政策 | laissez-faire 【lèsei fέər】<br>フランス語から来ています。 |
| 保護主義, 保護貿易 | protectionism<br>保護貿易主義者 protectionist |
| 輸入を妨げる | prevent imports<br>妨害する ① hinder ② impede |
| 並行輸入 | parallel import |
| 計画経済 | planned economy<br>市場経済 market economy |
| 二極化 | polarization<br>二極化する, 二極化させる polarize<br>polar は「極の」という意味で, polar bear といえば「北極グマ」のことです。 |
| 貿易外取引 | invisible trade<br>invisible はもともとは「目に見えない」という意味です。 |
| 互恵的貿易 | recíprocal trade<br>互恵, 相互依存 recipócity |
| 相互依存の | interdependent<br>相互依存 interdependence |

| | |
|---|---|
| 輸出と輸入はそれぞれ10億ドルと20億ドルでした。 | **Exports and imports were $1 billion and $2 billion respectively.**<br>この respectively「それぞれ」の使い方をしっかり覚えてください。ニュース英語ではよく使います。 |

## ◆ 収支

| | |
|---|---|
| 貿易収支 | trade balance<br>貿易不均衡 trade imbalance |
| バランスを保つ | keep in balance |
| 貿易黒字 | trade surplus<br>⇔ 貿易赤字 trade deficit |
| 過去最高の黒字を記録する | post a record surplus<br>post は厳密には「公表する, 公示する, 記入する」といった意味ですが,「黒字を記録する」というようなときにはよくこの post を使います。もちろん mark や,「発表する」の意味の report でもけっこうです。 |
| 拡大する貿易黒字 | widening trade surplus |
| 1億円の赤字を見込む | predict a deficit of 100 million yen |
| 経常収支 | current account |
| 経常黒字 | current account surplus<br>⇔ 経常赤字 current account deficit |

| | |
|---|---|
| 商社 | trading company [house] |
| 一年前に比べて40％アップ | up 40 percent from a year earlier<br>昨年に比べて compared to last year |
| 前年同月比 | year on year<br>前年同月比で<br>on a year-on-year basis |
| 一時的要因 | temporary factors<br>構造的要因 structural factors |

## ◆ 貿易摩擦

| | |
|---|---|
| 貿易摩擦 | trade friction<br>経済摩擦 economic friction |
| 関税 | tariff<br>報復関税 retáliatory [punitive] tariff |
| 関税化 | tariffication<br>例外なき関税化<br>**comprehénsive tariffication**<br>comprehensive は「包括的な」の意味です。 |
| 関税障壁 | tariff barrier<br>⇔ 非関税障壁 non-tariff barrier |
| 貿易障壁 | trade barrier |
| 規制 | ① regulation ② restriction<br>restriction は「制限」という感じです。<br>規制する ① regulate ② control |

## part 4 ● 貿易摩擦

| | |
|---|---|
| 規制緩和 | deregulation<br>規制緩和する<br>① deregulate<br>② relax [loosen, ease] the regulations<br>緩和 relaxation |
| 輸入制限 | import restriction<br>輸出制限 export restriction |
| 制限を設ける | put restrictions (on) |
| 自主規制 | ① self-imposed control<br>② voluntary restraint [rule]<br>自主規制する<br>control [limit] voluntarily |
| 輸出割当て | export quota |
| 原材料 | raw materials<br>天然ガス natural gas |
| 天然資源 | natural resources<br>日本は天然資源に乏しい。<br>Japan is poor in natural resources. |
| オイルショック | oil crisis |
| 付加価値 | added value<br>高付加価値製品<br>highly value-added product |

# ◆市場開放

| | |
|---|---|
| 自由化する | líberalize<br>自由化 liberalization |
| 市場開放 | market opening<br>コメ市場の部分開放<br>partial opening of the rice market |
| 市場をこじ開ける | pry the market open<br>この表現は「ドアをこじ開ける」ようなときも，pry the door open というように使えます。 |
| ダンピング | dumping<br>ダンピング防止税<br>(anti-)dumping duty |
| 新興市場 | emerging market |
| 急速に成長している市場 | rapidly growing market |
| 安価な労働力 | cheap labor |
| 産業の空洞化 | ① industrial hollowing<br>② hollowing-out of industry |
| ガット［関税および貿易に関する一般協定］ | GATT［General Agreement on Tariffs and Trade］<br>ウルグアイ・ラウンド<br>Uruguay【júərəgwèi】round |
| G7［7カ国蔵相会議］ | Group of Seven ［G7］<br>正式には Conference of Ministers of Group of Seven の通称です。 |

*part 4* ● 貿易摩擦

| | |
|---|---|
| WTO [世界貿易機構] | World Trade Organization [WTO]<br>日本はこの問題でWTOに裁定を求めた。<br>Japan appealed a ruling on this matter to the WTO. |

## ◆ 日米経済摩擦

| | |
|---|---|
| 日米構造協議 | Structural Impediments Initiative Talks<br>impedimentは「障害」のことです。 |
| スーパー301条 | Super 301 Article |
| その海外のデータには偏りがある。 | The overseas data are lopsided.<br>lopsidedは「偏った，不均衡の」という意味で，lopsided tradeというと「不均衡貿易」のことです。 |
| 商慣行 | business practices<br>不公平な unfair |
| (企業の)系列 | web of corporate alliances<br>webは「クモの巣」「放送局網」などのことです。 |
| 日本は経済力にふさわしい国際的な役割を果たすべきだ。 | Japan should play an international role commensurate with its economic power.<br>commensurate with「〜にふさわしい」の代わりにcompatible withやsuitable forなども使えます。「ふさわしくない」はunsuitableやinaptとなります。 |

| | また、「役割を引き受ける」にするなら **assume a role** となります。 |
|---|---|
| 大店法 | ① large-scale retail stores law<br>② laws restricting the opening of big new stores |
| 独占禁止法 | antimonopoly law<br>反トラスト法 antitrust law<br>「ひとり占めする」は **monopolize** といいます。**hog** という言い方もあります。The car hogs the road. といえば、「あの車は道の真ん中を走っている」という意味になります。 |
| 公正取引委員会 | Fair Trade Commission |

# ◆談合

| 入札 | bid(ding)<br>公開入札 open bid(ding) |
|---|---|
| 入札する | bid<br>入札者 bidder |
| 公示価格 | posted price |
| 入札手続き | bidding procedures<br>あらかじめ決められた手続きを踏む<br>follow the prearranged procedures |
| 談合 | ① bid-rigging<br>② informal price-fixing cartel |

①の rig は「(不正に) 操作する」という意味です。
**市場価格を操作する**
**rig market prices**

## ◆日本の企業社会

| | |
|---|---|
| 企業支配 | corporate governance |
| 財界 | business world<br>企業社会 corporate society |
| 財閥 | financial combine |
| 経団連 [経済団体連合会] | Japan Federation of Economic Organizations |
| 日経連 [日本経営者団体連盟] | Japan Federation of Employers' Associations |
| 経済同友会 | Japan Association of Corporate Executives |
| 日本商工会議所 | Japan Chamber of Commerce and Industry |
| 青年会議所 | Junior Chamber of Commerce |
| 非営利団体 | non-profit organization |
| 日本では零細企業が全体の9割以上を占めている。 | Small businesses account for more than 90% of all companies in Japan.<br>この account for「占めている」という表現も、ニュース英語ではよく使うのでしっかり覚えておいてください。たとえ |

ば他にも,「住宅産業からの収入が,総額の6割を占めている」というときには, **The income from the housing industry accounts for 60% of the total amount.** ということができます。

# part 5

# 為替相場

①円相場
②円高
③外貨準備高
④1ドル114円で取引されている
⑤口先介入
⑥協調介入に踏み切る
⑦政策転換
⑧通貨を切り下げる
これをあなたは英語でいえますか?

## ◆為替市場

| | |
|---|---|
| 外国為替市場 | foreign exchange market<br>外国為替相場 foreign exchange rate |
| 為替市場 | ① exchange market<br>② currency market |
| 変動相場制 | floating exchange rate system<br>固定相場制<br>fixed exchange rate system |
| 為替相場メカニズム | exchange rate méchanism<br>為替リスク exchange risk |
| 値上がり, 高騰<br>⇕ | appreciation<br>値上がりする, 高騰する appreciate |
| 値下がり, 下落 | depreciation<br>値下がりする, 下落する depreciate |
| 元に戻る | come around |

## ◆円相場

| | |
|---|---|
| 円相場 | yen quotation<br>絶えず(不規則に)変化する fluctuate |
| 円高 | ① yen's appreciation ② strong yen<br>円安 ① yen's depreciation<br>② weak yen |
| 外貨準備高 | foreign exchange reserve |

| | |
|---|---|
| 1ドル114円から115円で取引されている。 | The dollar is being traded between 114 yen and 115 yen.<br>「114円で」なら、**at 114 yen** となります。is being traded は、**is changing hands** といいかえることも可能です。もちろん「取引された」なら was traded, 「取引されていた」なら has been traded となります。 |
| 106円55銭から58銭で | between 106.55 ～ 58 yen<br>これは between 106 point five five and point five eight yen と読みます。数字の読み方については「日常会話編」part14のコラムでもやりました。 |
| 110円の値をつけた。 | The dollar fetched 110 yen. |
| ドルは105円を行ったり来たりしている。 | The US dollar hovers near 105 yen.<br>hover は本来「空を舞う(こと), ～のそばをうろつく(こと)」を意味します。 |
| ドルが円に対してわずかに安くなった。 | The dollar was slightly lower against the yen. |
| 小幅な動きをする | move within a small range |

## ◆ 通貨政策

| | |
|---|---|
| 介入する | intervene<br>介入 intervention |

| | |
|---|---|
| 口先介入 | verbal intervention |
| 協調介入に踏み切る | take a concerted [joint] step<br>協調利上げに踏み切る　take a concerted step to raise the rates |
| 遅まきながらも | belatedly |
| 政策転換 | policy reversal |
| 欧州通貨統合 | European Monetary Union [EMU] |
| (通貨を)切り下げる | ① devaluate　② devalue<br>切り下げ　devaluation |
| (通貨を)切り上げる | ① revaluate　② revalue<br>切り上げ　revaluation |

# part 6

# 株・株式市場

①株主総会
②総会屋対策を講ずる
③株主代表訴訟
④中堅の
⑤投機筋
⑥東証一部上場企業
⑦終値
⑧急騰する
⑨ボロ儲けする
⑩急落する
⑪損失補てん
これをあなたは英語でいえますか?

## ◆株

| | |
|---|---|
| 株(式) | ① stock ② share<br>発行済株式 outstanding shares |
| 株主 | ① stockholder ② shareholder |
| 株主総会 | ① stockholders' meeting<br>② shareholders' meeting |
| 総会屋 | (corporate) racketeer |
| 総会屋対策を講ずる | take preventive measures against racketeers<br>racketeer は動詞では「ゆする」の意味で、「ゆすり」は racketeering となります。<br>総会屋と手を切る<br>root out corporate racketeers |
| 商法 | Commercial Law<br>商法改正 revision of the Commercial Law<br>「改正する」は revise となります。 |
| 法に従って | in accordance with the law |
| 証券取引法 | Securities and Exchange Law<br>証券取引委員会 Securities and Exchange Commission [SEC] |
| 持ち株会社 | holding company |
| 株主代表訴訟 | class action by shareholders<br>class action は「集団訴訟」のことです。 |

## part 6 ● 株・株式市場

| | |
|---|---|
| 株式買入優先権, ストックオプション | stock option<br>ストックオプションを現金化する<br>**cash in stock options**<br>「スキャンダルで儲ける」というようなときも，この cash in を使って，cash in the scandal といいます。 |
| 証券会社 | securities firm [company, house]<br>野村証券 Nomura Securities |
| 株式仲介人 | stock [share] broker<br>仲介会社 brokerage (house) |
| 大手の | major<br>中堅の second-tier【tíər】 |
| 三大証券 | ① Big Three securities<br>② Big Three brokerage houses |
| 売買手数料, 売買委託手数料 | brokerage commission |
| 投資家 | investor<br>機関投資家 institutional investor |
| 投機筋 | speculator<br>投機的な speculative<br>投機する speculate<br>投機 speculation |
| 乗るかそるかの [一か八かの] 賭け | make-or-break bet |
| 信用取引 | ① deal [sale] on credit<br>② deal on margin |
| 裁定取引 | árbitrage |

| | |
|---|---|
| 銘柄 | ① stock name ② issue<br>主要銘柄 selected stock [issue] |
| 有価証券 | securities<br>額面 face value |
| 上場株 | listed stock<br>非上場株 unlisted stock<br>list は「上場する」という意味です。 |
| 上場企業 | listed companies<br>東証一部上場企業<br>listed companies on the Tokyo Stock Exchange's first section |
| 店頭株 | over-the-counter stock<br>優良株 blue chip |
| 優先株 | preferred stock<br>普通株 common stock |
| 株のもち合い, もち合った株 | interlocking stakes<br>interlock は本来「互いにかみ合う」の意味, stakes は「元手」の意味です。 |
| 持ち株比率 | ratio of the stock holdings |
| 東京三菱銀行の株を20％取得する | acquire 20% of (the stocks of) the Tokyo Mitsubishi Bank<br>取得 acquisition<br>持ち株を譲渡する divest my holdings |
| 買い注文 | buy order<br>⇔ 売り注文 sell order |
| 注文(する) | order<br>買い戻し buyback |

| | |
|---|---|
| 出来高 | ① volume ② yield<br>取引高 turnover |
| 売買代金 | selling［buying］price |
| 時価総額 | current share price<br>時価 current price |
| 値上がり株 | gainer<br>値下がり株 loser |

## ◆株価

| | |
|---|---|
| 株価 | stock price<br>相場 market price |
| 株式市場 | stock market |
| 東京証券取引所 | Tokyo Stock Exchange<br>ニューヨーク証券取引所<br>New York Stock Exchange |
| 連邦準備制度理事会 | Federal Reserve Board<br>連邦準備銀行 Federal Reserve Bank |
| 終値 | closing price<br>⇔ 始値 opening price |
| 高値 | high price<br>⇔ 安値 low price |
| 前日比 | from the previous day<br>前日比100円高［安］<br>up［down］100 yen from the previous day |

| | |
|---|---|
| ダウ平均[ダウ工業平均株価] | **Dow Jones industrial average** |
| ナスダック複合指数 | **NASDAQ composite index**<br>NASDAQ は National Association of Securities Dealers Automated Quotations の略です。 |
| 日経平均 | **Nikkei stock average**<br>平均して **on average** |
| 東証指数 | **TOPIX [Tokyo Stock Price Index]** |
| 最新の数字を見てみましょう。 | **Let's take a look at the latest numbers [figures].** |

## ◆ 値上がり

| | |
|---|---|
| 値上がりする | ① **rise** ② **surge**<br>surge は名詞では「波のうねり，高なり」のことです。 |
| 急騰する | ① **soar** ② **upsurge**<br>③ **shoot up** ④ **skyrocket**<br>soar, upsurge は名詞「急騰」としても使えます。「急騰」をさらに強めたいなら，steep upsurge などといいます。 |
| うなぎ昇りに上がる | **spiral**<br>spiral upward ということもあります。逆は，spiral downward となります。spiral は名詞では「らせん」のことで，spiral staircase といえば「らせん階段」 |

| | |
|---|---|
| | のことです。これも「日常会話編（上）」でやりました。 |
| 上昇傾向にある | buoyant【bɔ́iənt】<br>buoy は「ブイ，浮標」のことです。 |
| ピークに達する | hit the peak |
| ストップ高 | ① gains by its daily maximum limit<br>② gains by the daily trading limit<br>「ストップ高まで上がる」なら rise by its daily maximum limit などとします。 |
| ストップ安(まで下がる) | ① fall by its daily maximum limit<br>② fall by the daily trading limit |
| ボロ儲けする | ① make a killing<br>② scoop up<br>scoop は「大さじ」「すくう」などの意味です。特ダネで出し抜く「スクープ(する)」の意味もあります。<br>③ make money hand over fist |
| 分け前に預かる | get a cut of the action |
| 利にさとい奴だ。 | He knows which side his bread is buttered (on). |
| 配当 | dívidend<br>利回り yield【jiːld】<br>実質的利益 returns |
| 生み出す | generate |
| およそ | appróximately |
| 株価収益率 | price-earnings ratio【réiʃou】 |

# ◆値下がり

| | |
|---|---|
| 値下がりする | ① drop ② fall ③ decline ④ slide<br>15%値下がりする drop by 15% |
| 一時的に値を下げる,一時的下落 | dip |
| 下落する | shrink<br>shrink はもともとは「縮む」という意味です。 |
| 実質で | in real terms<br>名目で in nominal terms |
| 微調整 | ① fine tuning ② minor adjustment |
| 急落する | ① plunge ② tumble ③ plummet<br>④ take a (sharp) dive ⑤ nose-dive |
| 暴落(する) | crash<br>株価の暴落 stock market crash<br>この crash は車などが衝突するときや飛行機が墜落したときにも使います。clash は同じ衝突でも,「(意見,武力,利害など)が衝突する(こと)」です。一方,crush は「押しつぶす(こと)」で,crushing defeat といえば「惨敗」のことです。 |
| 引き金を引く | trigger |
| この出来事は安全ネットの必要性を浮き彫りにした。 | This incident highlighted the need for safeguards. |

*part 6* ● 株・株式市場

| | |
|---|---|
| 大損する | take a bath<br>もちろん「入浴する」の意味もあります。 |
| 損失 | loss |
| 損失補てん | compensation for (trading) losses |
| インサイダー取引 | insider trading |
| 内部の人間 | someone inside<br>内部情報 inside information<br>未確認情報 unconfirmed information |
| もみ消し(工作) | cover-up<br>もみ消す ① cover up ② hush up |
| 底を打つ | hit bottom |
| 反発する | ① rally ② bounce back ③ rebound |

## ◆市場の様子

| | |
|---|---|
| (相場の先行に関して)強気な人 | bull<br>本来は「雄牛」のことです。<br>⇔ 弱気な人 bear<br>「熊」のことですね。<br>ウォール街にまた弱気の虫が帰ってきた。<br>Bears are back again on Wall Street. |
| 強気な | bullish<br>⇔ 弱気な bearish |
| 好材料 | bullish factor<br>⇔ 悲観材料 bearish factor |

| | |
|---|---|
| 好材料は(相場に)織り込まれている。 | Bullish factors are reflected in market prices.<br>市場は悲観材料を反映している。<br>The market is reflective of bearish factors. |
| 今や悲観論が広がっているので… | Now that pessimism prevails… |
| 売買の材料 | trading incentives |
| 投資への熱意を失った。 | They soured on investing.<br>sour on で「～に対する熱意を失う」の意味になります。sour はもともとは「すっぱい, すっぱくなる」などの意味です。 |
| 警戒して | ① cautious  ② warily |
| 絶え間ない不安 | gnawing anxiety<br>gnaw は「～を苦しめる」の意味です。<br>高まる期待 growing expectation |
| 弱含みで推移している。 | We could see possible weakness. |
| 小康(状態) | lull<br>病気の「小康状態」のときは remission を使います。 |
| マーケットに活気がない。 | The market is inactive.<br>マーケットが混乱している。<br>The market is chaotic【keiátic】. |
| リスクをひどく嫌う社会 | risk-averse society<br>averse は「ひどく嫌って」という意味の形容詞です。 |

# ◆債券, 金融商品

| | |
|---|---|
| 債券 | bond<br>ジャンク・ボンド(紙クズ債券) junk bond |
| 発行する | issue |
| 社債 | ① corporate bond<br>② debenture (bond)<br>転換社債 convertible bond |
| 資本金 | capital |
| 増資<br>⇅ | capital increase<br>増資する increase its capital |
| 減資 | capital reduction<br>減資する reduce its capital |
| 米国債 | U.S. Treasury bond<br>ドル建て債 dollar-denominated bond<br>ドル建ての denominated in dollars<br>denominate は「特定の通貨単位で表示する」の意味で, 日本でいう「デノミ」は redenomination (downward) といいます。デノミは和製英語です。 |
| 償還 | redemption<br>未償還債 outstanding bond |
| 払い戻す | reimburse 【riːimbə́ːrs】 |
| デリバティブ[金融派生商品] | derivatives |

| | |
|---|---|
| 投資信託(会社) | investment trust [fund]<br>「オープンエンド型投資信託」は mutual fund といいます。 |
| 運用資産, 各種有価証券 | portfolio |
| 証券化 | securitizátion<br>証券化する secúritize |
| 先物取引 | ① future transactions<br>transaction は「取引」のことです。しばしば複数で使います。<br>② future contract |
| 仮定する | presume<br>仮定 presumption |

# part 7

# 税金

①国税庁
②公認会計士
③税金が高い
④累進課税
⑤分離課税
⑥非課税の
⑦税制優遇措置
⑧低所得者層
⑨減税要求
⑩脱税
これをあなたは英語でいえますか？

# ◆税金

| | |
|---|---|
| 国税庁〈日本〉 | National Tax Administration Agency<br>アメリカ国税庁<br>Internal Revenue Service [IRS] |
| 公認会計士 | certified public accountant<br>税理士 licensed tax accountant |
| 納税者 | tax payer<br>納税申告(書) tax return<br>「納税申告書」は tax forms ともいいます。 |
| 税負担 | tax burden |
| 直接税 | direct tax<br>間接税 indirect tax |
| 地方税 | local tax<br>住民税 residence tax |
| 所得税 | income tax |
| 法人税 | corporate tax<br>法人格 corporate status |
| 固定資産税 | (fixed) property tax<br>地価税 land price tax |
| 宅地 | residential land<br>商業地 commercial land |
| 相続税 | inheritance tax<br>贈与税 gift tax |
| 消費税 | consumption tax<br>売上税 sales tax |

| | |
|---|---|
| 税金が高い。 | Tax is high.<br>⇔ 税金が安い。Tax is low. |

# ◆課税, 免税

| | |
|---|---|
| 課税 | taxation<br>課税する ① put a tax (on)<br>　　　　　② tax (on) |
| 源泉課税 | taxation at the source<br>源泉徴収(税) withholding tax |
| 累進課税 | progressive tax(ation)<br>累進課税制度<br>progressive tax(ation) system<br>一率課税 flat tax(ation) |
| 分離課税 | separate taxation |
| 税率 | tax rate<br>最高税率 maximum tax rate<br>最低税率 minimum tax rate |
| 徴税 | tax collection<br>税収 tax revenue |
| 非課税の | tax-exempt<br>exempt は「免除する」という意味です。<br>「免除」は exemption。 |
| 免税の | ① tax-free ② duty-free |
| 税控除 | ① tax credit ② tax deduction<br>扶養控除 deduction for dependants |

| | |
|---|---|
| 減価償却 | depreciation<br>「(通貨の) 値下がり, 下落」という意味もありましたね。 |
| 税制優遇措置 | tax break<br>税制優遇措置を与える<br>provide tax breaks |

# ◆税制改革

| | |
|---|---|
| 税制改革 | taxation reform |
| 税制調査会 | ① Tax (System Research) Council<br>② Tax Commission |
| 中産階級, 中所得者層 | middle-income bracket<br>bracket は「階層」の意味です。<br>**低所得者層** low-income bracket<br>**高所得者層** high-income bracket<br>bracket(s)には「かっこ」の意味もありましたね。「日常会話編 (下)」でやりました。 |
| 増税 | ① tax raise ② tax increase<br>③ tax hike |
| 減税 | tax cut<br>**大幅減税** large-scale tax cut<br>**恒久減税** permanent tax cut |
| 減税要求 | demands concerning tax cuts |
| 脱税 | tax evasion |

## part 7 ● 税 金

| | |
|---|---|
| | 脱税する evade taxes |
| 脱税を阻止する | stop tax evasion |
| 抜け穴 | loophole<br>抜け穴をふさぐ<br>plug the (loop) holes |
| 税金回避地, 無税地 | tax haven |

haven は「避難所」の意味です。heaven「天国」とは違うので注意してください。

# part 8

# 相　撲

さて,経済用語をひととおり終えたところで,ひと息ついて,日本の国技である相撲の英語を勉強してみてください。日本固有と思われているものが意外に簡単な英語になります。

①相撲部屋
②親方
③まわし
④まげ
⑤立ち合い
⑥寄り切る
⑦投げを打つ
⑧休場する
これをあなたは英語でいえますか？

# ◆力士, 場所

| | |
|---|---|
| (大)相撲 | (grand) sumo wrestling【réslıŋ】<br>日本相撲協会<br>Japan Sumo Association |
| 力士 | (sumo) wrestler<br>相撲をとる, 格闘する<br>wrestle (with) |
| 兄弟子 | senior wrestler<br>弟弟子 junior wrestler |
| (相撲)部屋 | stable<br>stable は元々は「馬小屋」の意味で, 競馬では「厩舎」の意味で使います。<br>同部屋の力士 stablemate<br>やはり「同じ厩舎の馬」の意味もあります。 |
| 親方 | (stable) master |
| まわし | ① sash ② belt ③ loincloth |
| さがり | apron<br>化粧まわし ceremónial apron |
| まげ | topknot【tápnàt】 |
| 土俵 | ring<br>土俵入り ring entering ceremony |
| 徳俵 | ① straw ridge<br>ridge は「山の背, 細長い隆起」の意味です。 |

## part 8 ● 相撲

| | |
|---|---|
| | ② straw bales<br>bale は「俵」のことです。 |
| 土 | ① ground ② dirt |
| 清める | purify 【pjú(ː)ərəfài】<br>清め purificátion<br>この言葉は政治の世界の「みそぎ」の意味でも使います。 |
| 清めの塩をまく | throw [toss] (a handful of) salt to purify the ring |
| 弓取り式 | ① bow dance<br>② bow twirling ceremony |
| 行司 | referee 【rèfəfríː】<br>アクセントの位置に注意してください。 |
| 場所 | tournament |
| 番付(表) | ranking list<br>番付の上［下］の力士<br>sumo wrestlers in the higher [lower] echelon<br>echelon 【éʃəlàn】は「段階」の意味です。 |
| 関取 | top 50 sumo wrestlers<br>ハワイ出身の Hawaiian-born |
| 横綱 | ① grand champion<br>② highest rank wrestler<br>「横綱の地位」などというときの「**地位**」には **ténancy** を使います。 |
| 大関 | ① champion<br>② second-highest rank wrestler |

| | |
|---|---|
| 関脇 | ① junior champion<br>② third-highest rank wrestler |
| 小結 | junior champion second grade |
| 前頭一枚目 | maegashira No.1 |

## ◆取組

| | |
|---|---|
| 取組 | ①(wrestling) bout ② match |
| 対若乃花戦 | bout against Wakanohana<br>若乃花対貴乃花 bout between Wakanohana and Takanohana |
| 立ち合い | ① face-off ② initial charge |
| しゃがむ,仕切る | squat<br>立ち上がる start |
| 突進する | thrust forward<br>頭から当たる clash head-on |
| 右にかわる | jump to his right<br>引く pull off |
| 当たった瞬間に | the instant they made contact |
| はり手 | slap |
| まわしを取る | ① hold [snare, grip] the sash<br>② get hold of the sash |
| 上手 | outside grip<br>下手 inside grip |
| 前へ出る | go [move, charge] forward |

## part 8 ● 相撲

|  |  |
|---|---|
| 中へ入る | get inside |
| 決まり手 | winning trick [way] |
| 押し出す, 突き出す | push out |

「押し出す, 突き出す」にはこの他にも, thrust out, blast out, bump out, plow out などが使えます。

| | |
|---|---|
| 一気に | in a single burst |
| 寄り切る | force [muscle, walk] out<br>寄り切り forcing out |
| 土俵を割る | step out of the ring |

土俵際に押し込まれた。
He was shoved to the ring's edge.

| | |
|---|---|
| 押し倒す | push down<br>寄り倒す force down<br>引き倒す draw down |
| 投げ倒す | throw [toss] him to the dirt [ground] |
| 上手投げ | overarm throw<br>下手投げ underarm throw |
| 投げを打つ | try to throw (down) |
| 送り出す | drive out |
| つり出す | lift out<br>きめ出す lever out |
| はたき込む | slap down |
| 外掛け | outside leg trip |

## ◆勝敗

| | |
|---|---|
| (足の裏以外の)からだのどこかが土についたら負けです。 | When [If] any part of his body (except the soles of his feet) touches the ground, he loses. |
| 不戦勝(する) | win by default<br>default は本来「義務などの不履行」の意味で、スポーツでは「欠場(する)」のことです。 |
| 不戦敗 | loss by default<br>不戦敗する lose (a bout) by default |
| 今日の取組でケガをした。 | He was injured in today's bout. |
| ケガをしやすい。 | ① He is prone to injury.<br>② He is vúlnerable. |
| 休場する | ① pull out of the tournament<br>② withdraw from the tournament |
| まだ勝ち星のない | winless |
| 二敗目を喫する | suffer a second loss<br>二敗する suffer two losses |
| 六連勝 | six straight wins [victories] |
| 下す | down<br>「負かす、破る」の beat や defeat もよく使います。 |
| 星を五分に戻す | get his record back to even<br>「星」は record といいます。 |

*part 8* ◉ 相 撲

| | |
|---|---|
| 優勝争いをしている。 | He is in line for the championship.<br>優勝争いから脱落した。<br>**He was out of the running for the championship.**<br>was out の代わりに dropped out なども使えます。 |
| 優勝決定戦 | tie-breaker |
| 優勝する | win the tournament [championship]<br>賜杯 Emperor's Cup |
| 殊勲賞 | **Outstanding Performance Prize**<br>敢闘賞 Fighting Spirit Prize<br>技能賞 Technique Prize |

# part 9

# 選挙

①総選挙
②統一地方選
③国民投票
④補欠選挙
⑥小選挙区比例代表並立制
⑤格差を2倍以内に抑える
⑦現職の
⑧新人候補
⑨本命
⑩公約
⑪企業献金
⑫出口調査
これをあなたは英語でいえますか？

## ◆選挙

| | |
|---|---|
| 選挙 | election<br>総選挙 general election |
| 選挙制度 | election [electoral] system |
| 統一地方選 | local elections<br>知事選 gubernatórial election |
| 知事 | governor<br>東京都知事 governor of Tokyo |
| 市長 | mayor |
| 抜き打ち選挙 | snap election |
| 国民投票 | ①(national) referendum<br>「住民投票」も referendum といいます。<br>② plebiscite【plébəsàit】 |
| 選挙権 | ① suffrage<br>普通選挙権 universal suffrage<br>婦人参政権 women's suffrage<br>② right to vote |
| 被選挙権 | ① eligibility for election<br>② right to stand for office |

## ◆アメリカの選挙

| | |
|---|---|
| 大統領選 | presidential election<br>予備選挙 primary |

| | |
|---|---|
| 大統領選は4年に1回行われる。 | The presidential election takes place every four years. |
| 中間選挙 | midterm election<br>補欠選挙 by-election |
| 共和党 | Republican Party<br>Grand Old Party [GOP] ということもしばしばあります。<br>共和党員 Repúblican |
| 民主党 | Democratic Party<br>民主党員 Démocrat |
| 無党派(の),無所属(の) | ① independent ② nonpartisan<br>無党派層 ① independent voters<br>② unaffiliated voters<br>affiliate は「仲間に入れる,友好関係を結ぶ」などの意味です。「支店,支局」の意味もあります。「日常会話編(下)」でやりましたね。 |
| 党大会 | convention<br>党員集会 caucus 【kɔ́ːkəs】 |

## ◆日本の選挙

| | |
|---|---|
| 選挙管理委員会 | Election Control Commission |
| 公職選挙法 | Public Offices Election Law<br>公職選挙法違反 violation of the Public Offices Election Law<br>改正 revision |

| | |
|---|---|
| 選挙違反 | election irregularities<br>連座制 guilt [guilty] by association |
| 小選挙区(制) | single-seat constituency (system)<br>中選挙区 multi-seat constituency |
| 比例代表制 | proportional representation system |
| 小選挙区比例代表並立制 | single-seat constituency combined with the proportional representation system |
| 選挙区 | ① constituency<br>constituency には「有権者」の意味もあります。他に「顧客層」の意味もあります。<br>② election [electoral] district |
| 小選挙区の区割りをする | demarcate the electoral districts<br>区割り demarcation |
| 格差 | disparity |
| 格差を2倍以内に抑える | curb the disparity below two<br>経費などを抑えるときと同じように curb という言葉を使います。 |
| 過疎の | underpopulated<br>過密の densely-populated |
| 人口流出 | population outflow<br>人口流入 population inflow |

## ◆立候補, 候補者

| | |
|---|---|
| 大統領選に立候補する, 出馬する | run for the presidency<br>衆院選に立候補する, 出馬する<br>run for the House of Representatives |
| 候補者 | candidate |
| 党公認候補 | party-endorsed candidate |
| 党推薦候補 | ① party-backed candidate<br>② party-supported candidate<br>③ party-recommended candidate |
| 現職の | ① incúmbent ② sitting |
| 新人候補 | newcomer<br>新参者（political）novice【nάvis】 |
| 世間知らず | schmuck【ʃmʌk】 |
| 最有力候補, 本命 | front-runner<br>泡沫候補 fringe candidate<br>fringe は「(外)縁」のことです。 |
| 有力な候補 | ① strong [hopeful] candidate<br>② favorite<br>非常に有力な候補 heavy favorite |
| 当選確実な人, 大本命 | shoo-in<br>2位, 次点者 runner-up |
| 競う, 争う | vie with him<br>vie は進行形が vying となることに注意してください。もちろん compete なども使えます。 |

| | |
|---|---|
| 対立候補 | ① opponent ② contender ③ contestant |
| 指名候補 | nominée<br>指名する nóminate<br>指名 nominátion |
| 副大統領候補 | running mate |
| 候補者名簿 | slate of candidates |

## ◆選挙運動

| | |
|---|---|
| 選挙運動 | (election) campaign<br>選挙参謀 campaign manager |
| 事前運動 | pre-election campaign<br>予備的な exploratory |
| 戸別訪問 | ① home-to-home canvas<br>② door-to-door visits<br>「日常会話編」でもやったように, ここでも「(〜を) する」といいたいときは, carry out や conduct が使えます。 |
| 自分を売り込む | pitch himself<br>自画自賛する, ひけらかす<br>toot [blow] his horn |
| 遊説する | go on the stump<br>stump は「木の切り株」のことです。 |
| 草の根, 基盤 | grass roots |
| 地方を遊説する | barnstorm |

## part 9 ● 選 挙

| | |
|---|---|
| | 地方遊説 barnstorming |
| 演説の練習をする | rehearse a speech<br>rehearse はもちろん劇などの練習をするときにも使います。 |
| 応援演説 | pep talk<br>熱弁をふるう演説者 tub-thumper<br>thump は「強くたたく」という意味です。 |
| 演壇で | on the platform<br>教会の説教壇 pulpit |
| 決起集会, 気勢を上げる集会 | pep rally |
| 選挙事務所 | campaign headquarters |
| 公約 | ① pledge  ② campaign promise<br>公約する pledge<br>誓約, 誓う vow |
| 強調する | stress |
| 若い女性に照準を合わせる | zero in on young women<br>focus on も使えます。 |
| (プロの手による)イメージチェンジ | makeover |
| 資金集め | fund-raising<br>資金を集める fund-raise<br>資金調達者 fund-raiser |
| 献金 | donation<br>献金する donate |
| 企業献金 | ① corporate donation<br>② political donations by companies |

| | |
|---|---|
| 金権選挙 | bankrolled election |
| 金がたっぷりある。 | He is flush with money. |
| | 対立候補より多く金を使う |
| | outspend the opponent |
| 資金不足の | underfinánced |

## ◆世論調査

| | |
|---|---|
| 支持者 | ① supporter ② backer |
| 支持する | ① support ② back ③ endorse |
| 徹底して支持する | back him to the hilt |
| | hilt は「剣のつか」のことです。 |
| 支持 | ① support ② endorsement |
| | 彼の支持を取りつける |
| | pick up his endorsement |
| 熱心な | ① avid ② eager |
| 有権者 | constituency |
| | 「(一人ひとりの)有権者」を指していうときは, constituent や éligible voter という言葉を使います。eligible は「資格がある」という意味です。 |
| 選挙民 | ① eléctorate ② voters |
| | 選挙人名簿 voters' list |
| 国勢調査 | national census |
| | 国勢調査局 |
| | Census Bureau 【bjú(ː)ərou】 |

| | |
|---|---|
| 人口統計 | demógraphy<br>人口統計の demográphic |
| 世論調査 | (public opinion) poll<br>surveyという言葉を使うこともあります。 |
| 世論調査員 | pollster |
| アンケート(用紙) | ① questionary ② questionnaire |
| 出口調査 | exit poll |
| 無作為抽出 | random sampling<br>無作為に at random |
| 回答者 | respondent |

## ◆投票

| | |
|---|---|
| 投票 | vote<br>「投票する」vote (for) という動詞としても使えます。 |
| 棄権する | abstain (from voting)<br>棄権 abstention |
| 投票用紙 | ballot<br>投票する cast his ballot |
| 投票率 | (voter) turnout (rate)<br>高い投票率 high (voter) turnout |
| 雨で予想外に低い投票率になった。 | The rain brought about an unexpected low (voter) turnout. |
| 不在者投票 | absentee voting |

| | |
|---|---|
| 信任投票 | confidence vote<br>⇔ 不信任投票 nonconfidence vote |
| 接戦の | neck and neck with him |
| 大接戦 | dead heat<br>大接戦を演じる ① dead-heat ② run a dead heat |
| 私のほうが優勢だ。 | I have an edge over him. |

## ◆ 選挙結果

| | |
|---|---|
| 選挙結果は今日中に判明するでしょう。 | The election results will be known by midnight. |
| (結果は)まだわからない。 | It remains to be seen.<br>この表現はニュース英語ではよく使うのでしっかり覚えておいてください。 |
| 開票 | vote［ballot］counting<br>開票する count the votes |
| 開票結果 | election returns<br>票のごまかし vote rigging<br>rig は，票や価格などを「(不正に) 操作する」という意味でしたね。 |
| 集計 | tally<br>開票結果を集計する<br>tally up the election returns |
| 有効な | valid<br>⇔ 無効な ① invalid ② void |

## part 9 ● 選挙

| | |
|---|---|
| 1万票獲得する | ① garner 10,000 votes<br>② rack up 10,000 votes |
| 当選する | win<br>落選する lose |
| 議席を得る | win a seat<br>⇔ 議席を失う lose a seat |
| 負かす | beat |
| 無効とする | ① nullify ② annul【ənʌ́l】<br>無効 nullification |
| 当選を無効にする | strip him of his elected post<br>strip A of B で「AからBを剥奪する」の意味になります。 |
| 票差 | margin |
| 大差で | by a great [big, wide] margin<br>小差で by a small [narrow] margin<br>margin には「縁, 余白」の意味もあり, marginal は「縁の, 辺境の」の意味です。 |
| 地滑り的勝利 | landslide victory<br>完勝 sweeping victory |
| 僅差の勝利 | wafer-thin victory<br>wafer は「ウェハース」のことです。 |
| 惨敗 | crushing defeat |
| 決選投票 | runoff(vote, election) |
| 過半数 | majority<br>絶対過半数 absolute majority<br>過半数すれすれ bare majority |

| | |
|---|---|
| 自民党は過半数に2議席足りない。 | ① The LDP is two seats short of a majority.<br>② The LDP lacks two seats to be in a majority. |
| 50議席を確保する | secure 50 seats<br>議席を100まで伸ばす<br>increase its seats to 100 |
| この結果には決して満足していない。 | They are by no means satisfied with the outcome.<br>by no means で「決して〜でない」の意味になります。 |

# part 10

# 政治・政党

①立憲君主制
②政権に就く
③組閣する
④連立政権
⑤右派
⑥ハト派
⑦革新政党
⑧幹事長
⑨一枚岩の
⑩主流派
これをあなたは英語でいえますか？

# ◆ 政体

| | |
|---|---|
| 共和国 | republic<br>共和国への移行 shift to a republic |
| 王国 | kingdom<br>王位, 王座 throne<br>王朝 dynasty【dáinəsti】 |
| 王位に就く | come to the throne<br>王座にのぼる<br>mount [ascend] the throne<br>日本の皇位のことは, 菊の紋章からしばしば Chrysanthemun Throne といわれます。 |
| 王の | regal<br>王権 regal power |
| 戴冠式 | coronation |
| 王位継承 | succession to the throne<br>継承推定相続人 heir apparent |
| 王位を継承する | succeed to the throne<br>王位を継ぐ inherit the throne |
| 退位 | abdication<br>退位する abdicate |
| 君主国, 君主制 | mónarchy<br>立憲君主制 constitutional monarchy |
| 君主 | monarch<br>絶対君主 absolute monarch |

## part 10 ● 政治・政党

| | |
|---|---|
| 血は水よりも濃い。 | Blood is thicker than water. |
| 絶対主義 | absolutism<br>**相対主義** relativism<br>アインシュタインの「相対性理論」は，relativity といいます。 |
| 連邦 | ① federation<br>マレーシア連邦 the Federation of Malaysia<br>② union<br>(旧)ソ連邦 the Soviet Union<br>③ commonwealth<br>英連邦 the (British) Commonwealth of Nations |
| 連邦政府 | federal government |
| 首長国 | emirate 【ímərət】<br>**首長** emir 【imíər】 |
| 独裁制,独裁政権 | ① dictatorship<br>**独裁者** díctator<br>② autócracy |
| 専制政治 | déspotism<br>**圧政,暴政** tyranny |
| 言論の自由 | freedom of speech<br>**報道の自由** freedom of the press |
| 支配者 | ruler |
| 軍事政権 | military regíme<br>regime は「体制」のことです。 |

| | |
|---|---|
| 暫定政権, 臨時政権 | ① provisional government<br>「暫定予算」は provisional budget といいます。<br>② caretaker government<br>③ ínterim government |
| 暫定軍事政権 | junta【húntə, hʌ́ntə】<br>「フンタ」または「ハンタ」と発音します。 |
| 弱体政権 | feeble government<br>feeble は「弱々しい」の意味です。<br>死に体の móribund |
| 傀儡政権(かいらい) | puppet regime<br>puppet は「あやつり人形」のことです。 |
| 主権 | sovereignty【sávərənti】<br>「サヴリンティ」と発音します。 |
| 元首 | head of state |
| 国旗 | national flag<br>国歌 national anthem |

# ◆主義

| | |
|---|---|
| 民主主義 | demócracy<br>民主主義者 démocrat |
| 資本主義 | cápitalism<br>資本主義者, 資本家 capitalist |
| 共産主義 | cómmunism<br>共産主義者 communist |

*part 10* ● 政治・政党

| | |
|---|---|
| 社会主義 | sócialism<br>社会主義者 socialist |
| 国家主義, 民族主義 | nátionalism<br>国家主義者, 民族主義者 nationalist |
| 全体主義 | totalitárianism<br>全体主義者 totalitarian |
| 原理主義 | fundaméntalism<br>原理主義者 fundamentalist |

## ◆アメリカの政体

| | |
|---|---|
| 大統領 | President<br>副大統領 Vice President<br>中国の「国家主席」も President です。「総書記」は General Secretary です。 |
| 就任 | inauguration 【inɔːgjəréiʃən】<br>就任式 inauguration ceremony<br>就任させる ináugurate |
| 宣誓 | oath 【ouθ】<br>宣誓する swear |
| 4年の任期 | four-year ténure |
| 前任者をたたえる | pay homage [tribute] to his predecessor<br>homage は【hámidʒ】と発音します。homage も tribute も「尊敬の念, 敬意」の意味です。 |

| | |
|---|---|
| | ～に敬意を表して in honor of |
| クリントン政権 | **Clinton administration** |
| 政権に就く | **come into [to] power**<br>政権に返り咲く return to power |
| 政権を握っている | **hold the reins of government**<br>rein は「手綱」のことです。<br>政権を握る<br>**take over the reins of government** |
| 移行 | **transítion**<br>一時的な tránsient |
| 大統領執務室 | **Oval Office**<br>oval は「楕円形の」という意味で，部屋が楕円形であることから生まれた名称です。 |
| 側近, 大統領補佐官 | **aide** 【éid】<br>aid「援助，助力者，助手」とは違うので注意してください。 |
| 側近の人々, 取りまき | **entourage** 【à:nturá:ʒ】 |
| 大統領報道官 | **press secretary** |
| 長官 | **secretary**<br>副長官 deputy secretary |
| 国務長官 | **Secretary of State** |
| 司法長官 | **Attorney General**<br>アメリカではほとんどの省の長官には secretary が使われますが，司法長官はこのように呼ばれます。 |

*part 10* ● 政治・政党

| | |
|---|---|
| 大統領特権 | presidential prerogative |
| 罷免する, 解任する | ① remove [dismiss, discharge] him from the office<br>② throw him out of the office<br>罷免, 解任 ① removal ② dismissal ③ discharge |
| 弾劾する | impeach<br>弾劾 impeachment |
| 独立検察官 | independent counsel |

## ◆日本の政体

| | |
|---|---|
| 首相 | prime minister<br>副首相 deputy prime minister<br>首相代理 acting prime minister |
| 首相の座に就く | assume the post of prime minister<br>「政権に就く」は come into [to] power でしたね。 |
| 内閣 | cabinet |
| 組閣する | organize a cabinet |
| 内閣改造 | cabinet reshuffle [reshuffling] |
| 内閣官房長官 | chief cabinet secretary |
| 大臣 | minister<br>長官 director general |
| 大臣を任命する | appoint ministers |

101

| | |
|---|---|
| 大臣の職 | **portfólio**<br>portfolio には「有価証券」の意味もありましたね。 |
| 無任所大臣 | **minister without portfolio** |
| 甘言で手に入れる | **scrounge**【skráundʒ】 |
| ポストをめぐるえこひいき | **cronyism**【króuniizm】 |
| 実権のない役職[人], 役立たず | **lame duck**<br>文字通りにいえば「足の不自由なあひる」ということです。 |
| 次官 | **deputy minister** |
| 事務次官 | **administrative vice minister** |
| 政府高官 | ① **government official**<br>② **senior official** |
| 連立政権 | **coalition (government)**<br>連立内閣 coalition cabinet |
| (内閣)支持率 | **approval rate (for the cabinet)**<br>不支持率 non-approval rate |
| 大衆, 庶民 | ① **populace** ② **masses**<br>一般大衆 general public |
| 不平不満 | **rumblings**<br>複数で使います。rumble はもともとは「ガラガラ (ゴロゴロ) 音を立てる」という意味です。<br>もちろん complaint ともいいます。 |
| 不満を抱いた, 不満な | **disgruntled** |

## ◆保守, 革新

|  |  |
|---|---|
| 保守的な | conservative<br>保守主義 conservatism |
| リベラルな, 自由主義の | liberal<br>自由主義 liberalism<br>自由主義者 liberalist<br>libertarian は「自主独立主義者」のことです。 |
| 急進的な | radical<br>穏健な ① moderate<br>　　　　② level-headed |
| 漸進主義 | incrementalism |
| 中立の | neutral【njúːtrəl】<br>中立主義 neutralism<br>中立にとどまる remain neutral |
| 中立 | neutrality<br>非武装中立 unarmed neutrality |
| 非政治的な | ① nonpolitical ② apolitical |
| 右派, 右翼 | right wing<br>左派, 左翼 left wing |
| 中道派 | centrist<br>中道政権 centrist government<br>中道主義 centrism |
| 中道左派(の) | center-left<br>極左(の) ultraleft |

| | |
|---|---|
| ハト派 | dove |
| | ハト派の dovish |
| タカ派 | hawk |
| | タカ派の hawkish |
| | 頑迷なタカ派 diehard hawk |
| 強硬派 | hardliner |
| (運動などの)先頭, 指導者 | vanguard |
| | vanguard には「軍隊の前衛」の意味もあります。 |
| あなたの立場は誰にもわからない。 | Nobody knows where you stand. |
| コロコロ変わる | keep changing |

## ◆政党

| | |
|---|---|
| 政党 | political party |
| 綱領 | ① platform ② general principles |
| 信条, 見解 | ténet |
| 崇高な理念 | sublime idea [philosophy] |
| | 非常に高い目標 lofty goal |
| 教義 | dogma |
| 与党, 政権党 | ① ruling party [power] |
| | ② party in power |
| | ⇔ 野党 opposition party |
| 党利党略, 党派主義 | partyism |

part 10 ● 政治・政党

| | |
|---|---|
| ミニ政党 | mini-party<br>弱小政党 fringe party |
| 超党派(の) | bipartisan 【baipάːrtəzn】<br>「無党派(の)，無所属(の)」は independent か nonpartisan でしたね (p.85)。 |
| 革新政党 | reformist party<br>中道政党 centrist party |
| 自由民主党 | Liberal Democratic Party [LDP]<br>民主党 Democratic Party |
| 社会民主党 | Social Democratic Party<br>共産党 Communist Party<br>公明党などはニュース英語ではそのまま固有名詞として Komei Party といいます。 |
| 正真正銘の(誠実な)党員 | bona fide member<br>事実上の de facto |

## ◆ 自民党

| | |
|---|---|
| 自民党総裁 | ① president ② leader<br>副総裁 vice president |
| 総裁選 | leadership election |
| 幹事長 | secretary general<br>副幹事長 deputy secretary general |
| (社会党などの)委員長 | chairman |

| | |
|---|---|
| 政調会長 | ① chief policy planner<br>② chairman of the Policy Affairs Research Council |
| 総務会長 | chairman of the General Council |
| 国会対策委員長 | ① chairman of the (LDP) Diet Affairs Committee<br>② Parliamentary Affairs Chairman |

## ◆派閥

| | |
|---|---|
| 派閥 | faction<br>「学閥」は academic clique でしたね。「日常会話編（下）」でもやりました。「軍閥」は military clique といいます。<br>派閥主義 factionalism |
| (人などの)群れ | ① throng ② herd ③ horde<br>群集心理 herd instinct |
| 一枚岩 | mónolith<br>一枚岩の monolíthic |
| 同胞 | brethren |
| 金権の | venal【víːnl】<br>金権体質 venálity |
| 金権政治 | plutocracy【pluːtákrəsi】<br>「プルータクラシー」と発音します。<br>金権政治家 plútocrat |
| (豊富な)金脈 | bonanza |

## part 10 ● 政治・政党

| | |
|---|---|
| 政治不信 | mistrust in politics<br>政治不信が広がっている。<br>**Mistrust in politics is widespread [spreading, prevailing].**<br>信用できない untrustworthy<br>信用できる trustworthy【trʌ́stwə̀ːrði】<br>mistrustful は「(容易に)信用しない」, trustful は「信用しやすい」の意味になるので注意してください。 |
| 主流派 | mainstream faction<br>反主流派 anti-mainstream faction<br>非主流派 non-mainstream faction |
| (党内)左派 | leftist faction (within the party)<br>右派 rightist faction |
| 派閥争い | factional strife<br>派閥間の対決<br>showdown between two factions |
| 党内の激しい駆引 | intraparty jousting<br>joust はもともと「中世騎士の馬上試合(をする)」のことです。 |
| 有力な | ① dominant<br>② predominant<br>③ influential<br>有力な勢力 dominant power[group]<br>強力なグループ powerhouse |
| 中枢の | pivotal【pívətəl】<br>中枢 pivot |
| 不協和音 | discord |

| | |
|---|---|
| 内輪もめ, 些細なもめごと | storm in a teacup |
| 些細なことを大袈裟にする | make a mountain out of a molehill<br>molehill は元来は「モグラ (mole) 塚」のことです。<br>空騒ぎ much adó about nothing |
| 分裂する | ① break apart ② split<br>分裂 ① disruption ② split |
| 数で上回る | outnumber<br>The leftist faction outnumbered the rightist one.「数の上で党内左派が右派を上回った」のように使います。 |

## ◆長老

| | |
|---|---|
| 長老, 元老 | ① senior statesman<br>② patriarch 【péitriàːrk】<br>家父長制 patriarchy |
| 精力的な | strenuous |
| 元気いっぱいの | exuberant 【igzúːbərənt】<br>若返らせる rejuvenate<br>甦らせる, 甦る revive |
| 気が若い | young at heart |
| おせっかい好きな | officious<br>気むずかしい ① dour ② cranky |
| 実力者 | pótentate |

## part 10 政治・政党

|  |  |
|---|---|
|  | 導師 guru |
|  | 巨人 ① titan ② behemoth【bihíːməθ】 |
| 最高の人, 物 | superlative |
|  | 最高の, 至上の paramount |
| 大物 | ① big shot ② kingpin ③ magnet |
|  | 大立者 mogul【móugəl】 |
| 政治的影響力 | clout |
|  | 政治的影響力を高める |
|  | enhance his clout |
| 後光 | halo【héilou】 |
| 卓越した | éminent |
| 尊敬すべき | venerable |
| 欠点のない | impéccable |
|  | peccable は「罪を犯しやすい」という意味になります。 |
| 不抜の忍耐力 | dogged perseverance |
|  | dogged は「犬のようにひるまず食い下がる」という感じです。perseverance は【pə̀ːrsəvíərəns】と発音します。 |
|  | 労を惜しまない painstaking |
| 不屈の精神 | fortitude |
| 足元にも及ばない。 | I can't hold a candle to him. |
| 見習う | take a page from his book |
| 驚異的な実績 | ① staggering accomplishment |
|  | ② staggering achievement |
|  | stagger は「よろめく」という意味です |

が、他に「たじろぐ, たじろがす」という意味もあり、ここでの staggering は「（人を）たじろがせるほどの」という意味になります。

| | |
|---|---|
| 勇退する | **bow out** |
| 権力にしがみつく, 執着する | **cling to power** |
| マンネリだ。 | **He is ［has got］ stuck in a rut.**<br>rut は「わだち」のことです。 |

# part 11

# 権力闘争

①権力闘争
②主導権
③求心力
④急先鋒
⑤日和見を決め込む
⑥一匹狼
⑦冷遇する
⑧難局
⑨立場が逆転した
⑩五十歩百歩だ
これをあなたは英語でいえますか？

## ◆主導権

| | |
|---|---|
| 権力闘争 | power struggle |
| 主導権 | initiative |
| 主導権を握る | gain [take, have] the initiative<br>主導権を失う lose the initiative |
| 主導権争い, 綱引 | tug-of-war<br>本来は「運動会の綱引」のことです。<br>主導権争いをする have a tug-of-war |
| 指導力を発揮する | exercise leadership |
| 政治的手腕 | political skills |
| 求心力 | centrípetal force<br>弱まる wane<br>次第に減少していく dwindle |
| 存在理由 | raison d'être【réizoun détrə】 |
| 急先鋒 | spearhead<br>本来は「槍の穂」のことです。 |
| 断固たる決意 | ádamant resolution |
| 問題外だ。 | It's out of the question.<br>的外れ wide off the mark |

## ◆根回し

| | |
|---|---|
| 根回しをする | lay the groundwork for it<br>舞台裏の behind-the-scene |

## part 11 ● 権力闘争

| 政治的な取引をする, 駆引をする | **dicker**<br>もともとは「値段の交渉をする」という意味から来ています。 |
|---|---|
| 取引をする | **make [cut] a deal** |
| 狸寝入りをする, 死んだふりをする | **play possum**<br>possum はフクロネズミのことで, 危険な目にあうと死んだふりをすることで知られています。<br>**とぼける play dumb** |
| 抱き込む | **embrace**<br>**甘言でつる cajole 【kədʒóul】** |
| 彼を抱き込もうと全力を尽くした。 | **We bent over backwards trying to embrace him.**<br>bend over backwards は「背中を後ろへそり返す」というのがもともとの意味です。 |
| 今やあなたは私の友なので… | **Now that you are my friend...** |
| 明日の百より今日の五十。 | **A bird in the hand is worth two in the bush.** |
| 彼の協力が不可欠だ。 | **His cooperation is imperative.**<br>imperative には doctor's imperative のように, 名詞として「医者の義務, 強制」などの意味もあります。 |
| 折り合いをつける | **come to terms with him** |

| | |
|---|---|
| 我々の勝利は彼が協力してくれたおかげだ。 | ① **We attribute our victory to his cooperation.**<br>attribute A to B は「Aの原因をBに帰する」という意味です。<br>② **Our victory stemmed [resulted] from his cooperation.** |
| 優勢になる | get the upper hand over the enemy<br>優位を取り戻す<br>regain the upper hand |
| 跳躍台, きっかけ | springboard |
| 地歩を得る | gain ground |
| 優位な側につく | jump [get] on the bandwagon<br>bandwagon は「パレードの先頭の楽隊車」の意味です。 |
| 流れ, 趨勢, 時流 | stream<br>時流に乗って with the stream<br>⇔ 時流に逆らって against the stream |
| 潮流 | torrent |
| 内情に通じている | privy (to)<br>privy【prívi】は「プリヴィ」と発音します。 |
| 同調して | in sync<br>同調しないで out of sync |
| 他のみんなに合わせるよ。 | **I'll conform to others.** |

*part 11* ● 権力闘争

# ◆ 傍観

| | |
|---|---|
| 日和見(ひよりみ)を決め込む。 | They are waiting to see which way the cat jumps.<br>様子を見よう。<br>Let's see which way the cat jumps. |
| 成り行きを見守る | test the waters |
| 決めかねている。 | He is of two minds. |
| 憶測が渦巻いている。 | Speculation is swirling. |
| 懐疑論 | skepticism 【sképtəsìzm】<br>懐疑的な skeptical |
| 最新のニュースを聞かせてくれ。 | Please fill me in on the latest news. |
| ニュースの要約 | wrap-up |
| 選り好みの許されない選択 | Hobson's choice<br>この表現は昔，客の選択を許さずに，馬小屋の出口に近いほうの馬から順番に貸していたイギリスの Thomas Hobson という人の名前から生まれました。 |
| 傍観する | ① look on ② stand by ③ sit back<br>傍観者 ① onlooker ② bystander |
| 目立たないでいる，低姿勢を保つ | keep a low profile<br>high profile は「高姿勢，際立って世間の注目を浴びること」，high-profile はその形容詞になります。 |

115

# ◆一匹狼

| | |
|---|---|
| 一匹狼 | **máverick**<br>自分の子牛にけっして焼印を押そうとしなかったテキサスの牧場主 Samuel A. Maverick の名から来ています。 |
| 異彩を放つ | **cut a figure** |
| 大評判をとる, あっと言わせる | **make a splash** |
| (胸をたたくほどの)大見栄 | **①chest-thumps ②chest-thumping**<br>thump his chest で「胸をたたく」という意味です。 |
| からいばり, こけおどし | **bluster**<br>「はったり」は bluff といいます。「日常会話編（上）」でやりましたね。 |
| 物議をかもす | **cause a stir** |
| 甘んじて屈辱を受ける | **eat humble pie**<br>humble は「謙虚な」の意味です。 |
| 毅然としている。 | **He keeps a stiff upper lip.**<br>唇をしっかりと噛みしめている感じです。 |
| 肘鉄を食わせる | **rebuff** |
| 釣り合わせる, 釣り合い | **counterbalance** |

*part 11* ● 権力闘争

# ◆危機

| | |
|---|---|
| 冷遇する | give [show] the cold shoulder to him<br>冷遇される get the cold shoulder |
| 寝返る,造反する | defect<br>造反者 defector |
| 裏切りかねない | treacherous 【trétʃərəs】<br>裏切り,背信行為 treachery |
| 信用ならない,人をだますような | deceptive<br>だます deceive |
| 恩をあだで返した。 | He bit the hand that fed him. |
| 思い当たる節があったら,そのとおりだ(真実を認めなさい)。 | If the shoe fits, wear it. |
| 本末転倒だ。 | You put the cart before the horse. |
| 巻き込む | ① implicate  ② involve  ③ embroil |
| 追い払う | oust |
| 出し抜く,裏をかく | outwit |
| 抹殺する,取り除く | obliterate |
| 敵に屈服する | succumb to the enemy |
| 反動 | backlash |
| 危機に瀕している。 | We are at stake.<br>stake は「賭け」という意味です。 |
| 岐路に立っている。 | We are at the crossroads. |

| | |
|---|---|
| 情勢が厳しくなった。 | The situation got tough. |
| 間近に迫っている | ① imminent ② impending<br>崩壊が間近に迫っている。<br>**The collapse is imminent.**<br>「崩壊」には **debacle** という言葉も使えます。 |
| 難局 | ① ímpasse ② straits<br>straits はしばしば複数で使います。もともとは「海峡」の意味で，この場合も通例，複数で使います。 |
| 重大な局面 | momentous phase ［stage］ |
| 前代未聞の | ① unprécedented ② unheard-of |
| 八方ふさがり, 麻痺状態 | gridlock<br>袋小路 cul-de-sac<br>迷宮 labyrinth【lǽbərìnθ】 |
| 落とし穴 | ① pitfall ② catch |

## ◆逆転, 変革

| | |
|---|---|
| 事態の打開の前触れになる。 | It heralds a breakthrough.<br>herald は「～の前触れになる，～を予告する」の意味です。 |
| 立場が逆転した。 | ① **The tables are turned.**<br>② **The shoe is on the other foot.** |
| 日本の政治を方向転換させる | turn around Japan's politics |

part 11 ● 権力闘争

| | |
|---|---|
| 変革期 | watershed |
| 画期的な出来事 | milestone |
| パラダイム,規範 | paradigm 【pǽrədàim】 |
| (思想などの)導入 | infusion<br>吹き込む infuse |
| 重大性を帯びる | take on immense importance<br>take on には, take on the burdens「重荷を背負う, 引き受ける」, take on him「張り合う」などの使い方もあります。 |
| 裏目に出る | backfire<br>裏目に出た。It backfired. |
| チャンスはまだいくらでもある。 | There are plenty more fish in the sea.<br>他にやることがある。<br>I have other fish to fry. |
| 冷静でいる | keep my shirt on |
| 仕方ないさ。 | That's the way it goes. |

## ◆ 論争

| | |
|---|---|
| 最も重要な問題 | meat-and-potatoes issue<br>meat and potatoes は「最も重要なもの」という意味です。肉とじゃがいもは共にアメリカ人の主食です。<br>火急の問題 pressing issue |
| 火中の栗, 難題 | hot potato |

| | |
|---|---|
| 難問 | **Gordian knot**<br>古代の王 Gordius によって結ばれた結び目のことです。<br>難問を解決する<br>**cut the Gordian knot** |
| 意見の分かれる問題 | **divisive issue(s)**<br>divisive は【diváisiv】と発音します。<br>込み入った **íntricate** |
| 問題の核心 | **crux of the matter** |
| 物事の核心をついた，本質的な | **nitty-gritty** |
| 問題に取り組む | **address**【ədrés】**the problem**<br>もちろん address には他に，「宛名を書く」「～に語りかける」の意味もあります。「宛名」など名詞で使うときは，発音が【ǽdres】ともなります。<br>「取り組む」には work on なども使えます。 |
| 沈思黙考する | **muse**<br>よく考える **dwell（on）**<br>物思いに沈んだ，考え込んだ **pensive** |
| 要点を繰り返す | ① **recap** ② **recapitulate**<br>要点の繰り返し ① **recap**　② **recapitulation** |
| 最優先する | **place priority on it** |
| 重視する | ① **attach importance to it**<br>② **give weight to it** |

*part 11* ● 権力闘争

| | |
|---|---|
| 懸念 | ① concern ② misgivings<br>misgivings はふつう複数で使います。 |
| 懸念を表明する | express concern (about)<br>懸念を抱いている。<br>I'm concerned about it. |
| つまらない喧嘩をする, 口論する | squabble<br>口論, 喧嘩 hassle |
| うるさい奴だ。 | He is vocal.<br>耳ざわりな abrasive |
| たきつける | flare up the issue |
| 論争を避ける | steer clear of cóntroversy<br>これはもちろん, avoid controversy ということもできます。 |
| 意見に反論する | counter his opinion<br>異議を唱える dissent<br>反ばくする refute |
| 反対者 | naysayer |
| 彼は完全に間違っている。 | He is all wet. |
| 自分のアイデアを押し売りする, 押しつける | tout his idea |

## ◆ 中傷合戦

| | |
|---|---|
| 中傷 | aspersion 【əspə́ːrʃən】<br>中傷する cast aspersions on him |

| | |
|---|---|
| 誹謗(ひぼう)する | detract<br>誹謗者 detractor |
| 非難する | ① reproach ② criticize<br>名指しで非難する<br>criticize him by name<br>公然と非難する decry |
| (名声などを)曇らせる, 色あせさせる | tarnish<br>色あせた tarnished |
| 延々たる攻撃演説 | tirade 【táireid】 |
| 間接的に中傷する | undermine・<br>undermineはもともとは「〜の下に穴を掘る」という意味で、そこから「徐々に衰えさせる」や「間接的に中傷する」といった意味が出てきています。 |
| 冒とくする | ① blaspheme 【blæsfíːm】 ② profane<br>冒とく ① blasphemy ② profanity |
| 不遜な | irreverent<br>思い上がった pretentious<br>反感を抱かせる off-putting |
| 無礼な言動 | affront<br>無礼な insolent |
| 品位を落とすような | ① degrading ② demeaning<br>品位 grade<br>品性 grace |
| でたらめ, たわごと | ① sham ② hókum<br>まったくの sheer |

*part 11* ● 権力闘争

| | |
|---|---|
| 的はずれの発言 | inept remark |
| 無分別 | indiscretion<br>無分別な indiscréet |
| 馬鹿げた, 笑いを誘う | ludicrous【lúːdəkrəs】 |
| 気色ばむ | bristle |
| 堪忍袋の緒が切れた。 | I've run out of patience. |
| 五十歩百歩だ。 | ① It is six and two threes.<br>② It is six of one and half a dozen of the other. |
| 便法, 都合のよい | expédient<br>ご都合主義 expediency |
| それとなくほのめかす | ① hint subtly ② imply<br>遠回しの言及 oblíque mention<br>oblique には「斜めの」という意味もあります。 |
| 暗示, ほのめかし | inkling |
| レトリック, 修辞 | rhétoric |
| 悪意のある, 害悪を及ぼす | malévolent<br>⇔ 善意に満ちた benevolent |
| 軽蔑的な | ① pejorative ② derógatory |
| 言い方にとげがあったことを詫びます。 | I apologize for my barbs.<br>barb は「辛辣な言葉, いやみ」の意味です。 |

# part 12

# 国会・法案

①三権分立
②衆参両院
③臨時国会
④臨時審議会
⑤盗聴法案
⑥国民的合意
⑦予算を均衡させる
⑧水増し請求
⑨利払い
⑩行政命令
これをあなたは英語でいえますか？

# ◆三権分立

| | |
|---|---|
| 三権分立 | division[separation] of three powers |
| 立法 | legislature 【lédʒislèitʃər】<br>立法府 legislative branch |
| 行政 | administrátion<br>行政府 admínistrative branch |
| 司法 | judiciary 【dʒuːdíʃièri】<br>司法府 judicial branch |

# ◆国会

| | |
|---|---|
| 国会 | ① Diet ② Parliament<br>国会議員 member of the Diet |
| 衆議院 | ① House of Represéntatives<br>② Lower House [lower house] |
| 衆議院議員 | ① Representative<br>② member of the lower house |
| 参議院 | ① House of Councillors<br>② Upper House [upper house] |
| 参議院議員 | ① Councillor<br>② member of the upper house |
| 衆参両院 | ① Lower and Upper Houses<br>② joint Diet |

*part 12* ● 国会・法案

| | |
|---|---|
| 衆議院議員を4期務める | serve four terms in the lower house |
| 議員, 立法者 | ① legislator ② law maker<br>legislate は「法律を制定する」の意味です。 |
| 政策立案者 | policy maker |

## ◆議会

| | |
|---|---|
| 本会議 | plenary 【plíːnəri】 session<br>議場, 議会 chamber |
| 通常国会 | ordinary session<br>臨時国会 extraordinary session<br>特別国会 special session |
| 会期 | session |
| 委員会 | committee<br>小委員会 subcommittee |
| 外交委員会 | foreign relations committee<br>「委員」は国会議員のときと同じように, member を使えばいいわけです。<br>予算委員会 budget committee |
| 審議会 | advisory council<br>専門委員会 panel |
| 臨時審議会, 特別審議会 | ad hoc council<br>ad hoc は「そのためだけの」という意味です。 |
| 地方議会 | local assembly |

| | |
|---|---|
| | 都議会 Metropólitan Assembly<br>県議会 prefectural assembly |
| 市議会 | city assembly<br>町議会 town assembly<br>村議会 village assembly |
| 市役所 | city hall　　村役場 village hall |
| 召集する | ① convene　② call<br>召集 convocation |
| 開会する | open（the session）<br>開会 opening |
| 休会する | adjourn【ədʒə́ːrn】（the session）<br>adjourn には「継続審議にする」という意味もあります。名詞の「継続審議」はadjournment。<br>休会 recess |
| 再開する | resume【rizúːm】<br>再開 resumption |
| 解散する | dissolve【dizálv】<br>解散 dissolution【dìsəlúːʃən】 |
| 閉会する | close（the session）<br>閉会 closing |

## ◆アメリカの議会

| | |
|---|---|
| アメリカ議会 | ① Congress　② Capitol Hill |
| 下院 | ① House of Representatives |

*part 12* ● 国会・法案

|  |  |
|---|---|
|  | ② Lower House [lower house] |
| 下院議員 | ① Representative<br>② Cóngressman [woman] |
| 上院 | Senate【sénit】<br>上院議員 Senator |
| 一般教書 | state of the Union message<br>アメリカの大統領が議会に提出する三大教書のひとつで，あとの二つは，「**予算教書**」Budget message と「**経済報告**」Economic report です。一般教書の state は「現状」のこと，Union は「連邦国家」，すなわち「アメリカ合衆国」のことを指しています。 |
| 一般教書演説をする | deliver his state of the Union message to Congress |

## ◆法案

| 法案 | bill<br>一括法案 package |
|---|---|
| 盗聴法案 | wire-tapping bill |
| 動議 | motion |
| 法案を提出する | submit a bill (to the Diet)<br>提出 submission |
| 審議する | delíberate<br>審議 deliberátion |

| | |
|---|---|
| 進行中の | ongoing |
| 法案を投票にかける | put the bill to a vote |
| 可決する | pass a bill<br>可決 passage |
| 承認する | approve<br>承認 approval |
| 法案が可決された。 | The bill was passed.<br>かろうじて narrowly |
| 法案が国会を通過した。 | ① The bill went through the Diet.<br>② The bill cleared the Diet. |
| 強硬に国会を通す | ram it through the Diet |
| 法案を成立させる | enact<br>法案は今国会中に成立する見通しです。<br>The bill is expected to be enacted during this session.<br>法案が成立した。<br>The bill was enacted. |
| 動議は可決されました。 | The motion was carried.<br>動議は否決されました。<br>The motion was lost.<br>もちろん carry の代わりに pass, lose の代わりに reject を使ってもいうことができます。 |
| 決議する | resólve<br>決議 resolútion<br>意志の堅い, 断固たる résolute |

## part 12 ● 国会・法案

| | |
|---|---|
| 採択する | adopt<br>採択 adoption |
| 否認する | disapprove<br>否認 disapproval |
| 否決する | reject<br>否決 rejection |
| 決定を覆す | override<br>override はもともと「蹂躙(じゅうりん)する」という意味で、「人権蹂躙」なら overriding human rights となります。<br>また overriding は形容詞として「最優先の」という意味にもなります。<br>最優先の課題 overriding problem |
| 拒否権(を発動する) | veto 【víːtou】 |
| 台無しにする | wash out the effort<br>狂わせる, 脱線させる derail |
| 保留にする | ① suspend<br>保留 suspension<br>② put it on hold |
| 未解決の, 懸案の | pending<br>懸案(事項) pending question<br>pending は前置詞として, pending the trial (裁判のあいだ) のように,「〜を待つあいだ」という意味でも使えます。 |
| 法案を棚上げする | ① shelve [table] the bill<br>② get the bill shelved |

| | |
|---|---|
| 白紙に戻す | clean the slate<br>slate は「石板」の意味です。 |
| 改正する, 修正する | amend<br>改正, 修正 amendment<br>「修正する」「修正」はそれぞれ modify, modification ともいいます。 |
| 修正を強く求める | solicit the amendment<br>懇請 solicitation<br>「強く求める」には他に urge も使えます。 |
| 憲法改正 | revision of the Constitution<br>改訂する revise |
| 正式な手続き | due process |
| 試案 | tentative plan |
| 国民的合意 | national consensus |

## ◆予算

| | |
|---|---|
| 予算(案) | budget (bill)<br>国家予算 national budget |
| 会計年度 | fiscal year |
| 主計局 | Budget Bureau<br>会計検査院 Board of Audit |
| 予算を監督する | oversee the budget |
| 一般会計 | general account |

## part 12 ● 国会・法案

| | |
|---|---|
| 歳入 ⇕ | révenue<br>収入 income |
| 歳出 | expénditure<br>支出 spending |
| 財政赤字 | budget deficit<br>⇔ 財政黒字 budget surplus |
| 累積赤字 | ① accumulated deficit<br>② cumulative【kjúːmjulətiv】deficit |
| 予算を均衡させる | balance the budget<br>均衡予算 balanced budget |
| 予算原案 | draft budget |
| 予算要求 | budgetary request |
| 概算要求枠, シーリング | budget ceiling |
| 予算折衝 | budgetary negotiátion<br>折衝する negótiate |
| 水増し要求 | padded request<br>水増し請求 padded bill<br>水増し padding<br>水増しする pad<br>pad は本来「当てもの」の意味で，動詞では「当て物をする，詰め物をする」という意味です。そこから「水増しする」という意味が出てきます。 |
| 予算審議 | budget deliberation<br>「審議する」は deliberate でしたね。 |

| | |
|---|---|
| 予算配分 | budget allocátion<br>配分する ① állocate ② allót |
| 見直し, 見直す | review |
| 予算修正 | budget modification<br>修正する modify |
| 暫定予算 | provisional budget<br>補正予算 supplementary budget |
| 予算削減 | budget reduction<br>予算を削減する reduce budget |
| 来年度の予算は緊縮型になる。 | Next year's budget will be tight. |
| 赤字国債 | ① deficit-covering bonds<br>② bonds to fill a revenue shortfall |
| 利払い | debt-servicing costs |

## ◆ 混乱, 紛糾

| | |
|---|---|
| 行き詰まる | come to a standstill<br>行き詰まり standstill<br>「行き詰まり」には他に standoff や deadlock も使えます。 |
| 滞らせる | stall |
| 混乱する | fall into disorder<br>混乱 disorder |
| 紛糾させる | ① tangle ② entangle<br>紛糾 ① tangle ② entanglement |

| | |
|---|---|
| 政治的紛糾を切り抜ける | hack a political tangle<br>てんてこまいの(生活) hectic (life) |
| 麻痺させる | ① paralyze ② cripple |
| 激しい抗議 | outcry |
| 不信任動議(案) | nonconfidence motion<br>不信任動議案をうまくかわす<br>head off a nonconfidence motion |
| 初めから決まっている結論 | foregone conclusion<br>既成事実 accomplished fact |
| 元に戻る | ① get back to normal<br>② return to normal<br>元に戻す ① get it back to normal<br>　　　　② return it to normal |
| 結論に達する | come to the conclusion |

## ◆法律

| | |
|---|---|
| 成文法 | státute [státutory] law<br>statute は「法令(書)」の意味です。 |
| 不文法 | common law |
| 条令 | ordinance<br>都道府県条令 prefectural ordinance<br>市条令 city ordinance |
| 条令を発する | issue [set forth] an ordinance<br>発布 issue |

| | |
|---|---|
| 条項 | provision |
| 大統領令 | presidential decree<br>布告する decree |
| 行政命令 | ① administrative order<br>② executive order |
| 公布する | ① proclaim ② promulgate<br>公布 ① proclamation<br>　　　② promulgation |
| 公式な発表 | official announcement<br>知らせる notify |
| 実施する,履行する | ① ímplement<br>履行 implementátion<br>② take [put] it into effect |
| 施行する | enforce<br>施行 enforcement |
| 発効する | ① take effect<br>② go [come] into effect<br>新しい法律は来月発効する。<br>The new law goes into effect next month. |
| 合法化する | ① make it legal ② legalize |
| 無効にする | ① make it illegal<br>② make it ineffective<br>③ strike down |
| 法律的に無効な | ① invalid ② (null and) void |
| 取り消す | ① revoke ② repeal ③ rescínd |

## part 12 ● 国会・法案

| | |
|---|---|
| | 取り消し ① revocation ② repeal ③ rescindment |
| 省略する | abbréviate |
| | 省略 ① abbreviátion ② omission |
| 凍結(する) | freeze |

# part 13

# 官僚・行政改革

①圧力団体
②請願
③族議員
④不正支出
⑤職務権限
⑥私腹を肥やす
⑦流用する
⑧縁者びいき
⑨縄張り争い
⑩地方分権を行う
これをあなたは英語でいえますか？

## ◆議員活動

| | |
|---|---|
| ロビー活動をする | lobby (for)<br>「根回しをする」は lay the groundwork for it でしたね。 |
| ロビー活動 | lobbying<br>ロビイスト lobbyist |
| 圧力団体 | pressure group<br>利益団体 interest group |
| 企業の圧力にひるむ | cave to corporate pressure<br>尻込みする cringe |
| 請願 | petition<br>嘆願する make a petition |
| 族議員 | special interest legislator<br>議員同士の慣れ合い logrolling |
| 受益者 | beneficiary |
| 気前よくもてなす | wine and dine |
| 助成金, 補助金 | subsidy 【sʌ́bsədi】<br>助成金[補助金]を支給する subsidize |

## ◆不正, 賄賂

| | |
|---|---|
| 賄賂 | ① bribe<br>贈収賄(事件) bribery scandal<br>② payoff |

## part 13 ● 官僚・行政改革

| | |
|---|---|
| | 金をつかませる pay off |
| 贈賄する, 買収する | ① give [offer] a bribe<br>⇔ 収賄する take [accept] a bribe<br>② bribe |
| あっせん利得 | influence peddling<br>あっせんする人 influence peddler<br>peddler はもともとは「行商人」のことです。 |
| 不正行為 | ① wrongdoing ② malpractice<br>③ irregularity ④ foul play<br>④の foul play には「反則」の意味もあります。<br>不正行為に注意を喚起する<br>bring attention to the wrongdoings |
| 不正支出 | spending irregularity |
| 疑惑 | ① allegation ② misgivings<br>③ suspicion |
| 違法行為 | misconduct<br>犯罪行為 misdeed |
| 汚職 | scandal |
| リベート | ① kickback ② rake-off<br>英語の rebate は「払い戻し, 割り戻し」の意味で, 日本語のように悪い意味はありません。 |
| 利権, 利益供与 | pork (barrel) |
| 職務権限 | administrative authority |

| | |
|---|---|
| | 権力[職権]の乱用<br>abuses of his power |
| 裏金 | slush fund |
| 公然の | overt<br>⇔ 秘密の covert |
| 隠す | cover up<br>隠匿 coverup<br>物を隠すのはもちろん hide です。 |
| 蓄財する | amass<br>蓄財 amassment |
| 横領する | ① embezzle ② usurp 【juːsə́ːrp】<br>横領 ① embezzlement<br>　　② usurpation |
| 私腹を肥やす | line his pockets |
| 流用する | divert<br>divert はもともとは「わきへそらす」という意味です。そこから「流用する」という意味が出てきます。<br>資金の流用 diversion of funds |
| 腐敗 | corruption<br>腐敗した corrupt |
| 腐敗して機能しなくなった | corrupt and incompetent |
| 醜聞 | muck<br>醜聞をあさる muckrake |
| 温床 | hotbed |

*part 13* ● 官僚・行政改革

| | |
|---|---|
| 縁者びいき | **nepotism**<br>近親者 **next of kin**<br>kin は「親族，一族，一門」などの意味です。**akin** というと「同族の，類似の」の意味になります。 |
| 信用を傷つける | **hurt his credit**<br>非難を招く，評判を落とす **disparage** |
| 社会通念 | **social norms** |
| 公明正大な | **righteous** |
| 連帯責任 | **joint responsibility** |
| 免責，責任逃れ | **impunity**【impjúːnəti】 |
| みそぎ | **purification**<br>「清め」と同じ言葉を使います。 |
| 市民オンブズマン | **citizen ombudsman[woman]** |
| 腐敗を一掃する | **stamp out corruption**<br>健全化する **sanitize** |
| 公職から退ける | **unseat him**<br>かわりに就任する **supersede him** |
| 厳しく罰する | **throw the book at him** |
| 救い主，救世主 | **savior** |
| 到来，出現 | **ádvent**<br>Advent と大文字になると，「キリストの降臨」を意味します。 |

# ◆官僚, 行政改革

| | |
|---|---|
| 官僚 | bureaucrat 【bjúərəkræt】 |
| 官僚主義 | buréaucracy<br>肥大化した官僚組織<br>bloated bureaucracy |
| 官僚的形式主義,<br>お役所流 | red tape<br>red tape とは「公文書を結ぶ赤い紐」のことです。<br>お役所流をやめる cut red tape |
| 縄張り | turf<br>縄張り争い turf battle |
| 行政改革 | administrative reforms<br>改革を擁護する<br>champion the reforms |
| 省庁 | ministries and agencies |
| 単純化する | simplify |
| 説明責任 | accountability |
| (整理)統合する | ① integrate ② consolidate<br>統合 ① integration<br>　　　② consolidation |
| 分離する | separate<br>分離 separation |
| 廃止する | abolish<br>廃止 abolition |

| 思いきった措置 | ① drastic action [measures]<br>② résolute action [measures]<br>measure は通例，複数で使います。 |

# ◆地方分権

| | |
|---|---|
| 地方自治 | regional autónomy<br>自治(権) autonomy |
| 地方自治体 | ① local government<br>② munícipal government |
| 地方分権 | decentralization<br>地方分権を行う decentralize |
| (地方への)権限委譲 | devolution<br>権限を委譲する devolve |
| 遷都 | relocation of the capital<br>首都機能移転<br>relocation of capital functions |
| 一極集中 | convergence<br>一極に集中した convergent |
| 都市のスプロール現象 | sprawl |
| 中核 | hub<br>社会の中核 social hub<br>「ハブ空港」のハブはここから来ています。 |

## コラム 省庁の名前

### 日本の省庁

| | |
|---|---|
| 法務省 | Ministry of Justice |
| 外務省 | (1) Ministry of Foreign Affairs<br>(2) Foreign Ministry |
| 大蔵省 | (1) Ministry of Finance<br>(2) Finance Ministry |
| 文部省 | Ministry of Education |
| 厚生省 | Ministry of Health and Welfare |
| 農林水産省 | Ministry of Agriculture Forestry and Fisheries |
| 通商産業省 | Ministry of International Trade and Industry |
| 運輸省 | (1) Ministry of Transport<br>(2) Transport Ministry |
| 郵政省 | Ministry of Posts and Telecommunications |
| 労働省 | Ministry of Labor |
| 建設省 | Ministry of Construction |
| 自治省 | Ministry of Home Affairs |
| 総務庁 | Management and Coordination Agency |
| 金融監督庁 | Financial Supervisory Agency |

「金融再生委員会」は Financial Reconstruction Commission といいます。

| 防衛庁 | Defense Agency |
| 経済企画庁 | Economic Planning Agency |
| 科学技術庁 | Science and Technology Agency |
| 環境庁 | Environment Agency |
| 国土庁 | National Land Agency |
| 宮内庁 | Imperial Household Agency |
| 気象庁 | Meteorological Agency |

## アメリカの省庁

| 国務省 | Department of State |
| 財務省 | Department of Treasury |
| 国防総省 | Department of Defense |

通称 Pentagon ともいいます。

| 司法省 | Department of Justice |
| 商務省 | Department of Commerce |
| 労働省 | Department of Labor |
| 農務省 | Department of Agriculture |
| 運輸省 | Department of Transportation |
| 保健福祉省 | Department of Health and Human Services |
| 教育省 | Department of Education |
| エネルギー省 | Department of Energy |
| 住宅都市開拓省 | Department of Housing and Urban Development |

　各省の大臣・長官は，日本では minister と director general，アメリカでは主に secretary を使います。固有名詞として使うときは，頭文字を大文字にします。

# part 14

# ニュービジネス・ニューテクノロジー

①先端技術
②リニアモーターカー
③特許権侵害
④海賊版
⑤液晶ディスプレイ
⑥データ処理
⑦情報の暗号化
⑧有望な市場
⑨新設企業
⑩小回りのきく
これをあなたは英語でいえますか?

## ◆先端技術

| | |
|---|---|
| 最先端技術 | state-of-the-art technology<br>先端技術 advanced technology |
| 新技術に遅れずについていく | keep up with the new technology |
| 基本原理 | postulate<br>定数 constant |
| 革新的な | innovative<br>革新 innovation |
| とてつもなく大きな影響[インパクト] | massive impact |
| 秘密研究開発部門 | skunk works |
| 新しい道の開拓者 | trailblazer<br>探究 quest |
| 頭脳流出 | brain drain |
| 目新しいもの | nóvelty<br>うまく工夫した機械装置 gadget |
| (新製品などの)氾濫 | deluge【déljuːdʒ】 |
| 実物の模型 | full-scale model |
| リニアモーターカー | ① linear motor train<br>② magnetic levitation train<br>levitate は「空中に浮き上がらせる」の意味です。 |
| 人間工学 | ergonómics |

part 14 ● ニュービジネス・ニューテクノロジー

| | |
|---|---|
| ファイバーオプティクス | fiber optics |
| 技術移転 | technology transfer<br>技術を(中国に)移転する<br>transfer technology (to China) |

## ◆ 特許, 知的所有権

| | |
|---|---|
| 特許(権) | pátent |
| 特許権侵害 | patent infringement<br>侵害する infringe |
| 著作権 | copyright<br>著作権法 copyright system |
| 知的所有権 | intellectual property |
| 海賊行為, 著作[特許]権侵害 | piracy<br>著作権侵害者, 著作権を侵害する pirate<br>海賊版 pirate(d) edition |
| テクノロジーが法律を追い越している。 | Technology has outpaced law. |

## ◆ コンピュータ

| | |
|---|---|
| そろばん | abacus 【ǽbəkəs】 |
| ノート型パソコン | laptop computer<br>laptop は「膝の上」の意味です。 |

| | |
|---|---|
| 集積回路 | íntegrated circuit [IC] |
| 半導体 | semiconductor |
| 電流 | electric current<br>直流 direct current<br>交流 alternating current |
| 直列 | series<br>並列 parallel |
| 静電気 | static electricity |
| 伝える | ① convey<br>コンベヤー conveyor<br>② transmit<br>伝導 transmission |
| 液晶ディスプレイ | liquid crystal display |
| 駆動装置 | operating system [OS] |
| 周辺機器 | peripheral equipment<br>peripheral は【pərífərəl】と発音します。 |
| データ処理 | data processing |
| 削除する | delete<br>削除 deletion |
| 挿入する | insert<br>挿入 insertion |
| アイコン | icon<br>クリックする click (on) |
| 閲覧ソフト | browser |

## part 14 ● ニュービジネス・ニューテクノロジー

| | |
|---|---|
| ホームページ | ① web site ② homepage |
| URL(ホームページのアドレス) | URL [Uniform Resource Locator] |
| インターネット検索ページ | ① portal (site) ② search engine<br>Yahoo や Excite などのことです。 |
| LAN | local area network [LAN] |
| 双方向の | interactive<br>相互作用 interaction<br>相互に作用する interact |
| 熟達した, 熟達者 | proficient<br>英語に堪能な proficient in English<br>技術的に熟達した<br>technically proficient<br>堪能さ, 熟達さ proficiency |
| コンピュータ2000年問題 | Y2K problem<br>Y2 は Year 2000のことで, K は Kilo の略で「千」を意味します。K はまた電算記憶容量の単位で2の累乗のうち1000に最も近い数も指します。<br>「2000年問題」には他に **millennium bug** のような言い方もあります。millennium は「千年 (の)」の意味です。 |
| コンピュータの欠陥 | ①(computer) glitch ② bug |
| コンピュータウイルス | computer virus 【váiərəs】<br>virus は「**ヴァイラス**」と発音します。 |
| 侵入する | ① penetrate ② intrude ③ interlope<br>侵入 ① penetration ② intrusion |

| | |
|---|---|
| 不法侵入(する) | trespass |
| コンピュータを無力にする | swamp computers |
| プライバシーの保護 | protection of privacy |
| 情報の暗号化 | encryption<br>暗号化する ① encrypt ② code |
| 暗号解読 | decryption<br>暗号を解読する ① decrypt ② decode |
| (クレジットカードなどを)読み取り機に通す | swipe<br>読み取り機 swipe machine |

## ◆ニュービジネス

| | |
|---|---|
| 有望な市場 | promising market<br>付属のマーケット ancillary market |
| 市場の隙間, 隙間市場 | niche【nítʃ】 |
| 現実的[実際的]なビジネス | down-to-earth business |
| 電子マネー | cybermoney |
| 成長[存続]しうるビジネス | viable business<br>存続可能性 viability |
| 急成長している, 増長している | burgeoning |

## part 14 ● ニュービジネス・ニューテクノロジー

| | |
|---|---|
| もしうまくいかなかったら… | If things don't work out...<br>もしうまくいったら…<br>If things work out...<br>if のあとは未来のことでも未来形を使わないことに注意してください |
| たぶんそうなるだろう。 | That will be the case. |
| 粘り強い企業家 | tenacious entrepreneur |
| 新設企業 | start-up<br>発展の可能性のある新設企業<br>seminal start-up |
| 潜在能力 | potential |
| 小回りのきく | nimble<br>機敏な agile【ǽdʒəl】 |
| 積極的な, 元気のいい | feisty【fáisti】 |
| 大躍進(で) | (in) quantum jump [leap]<br>quantum は「量子」「多量」などの意味です。 |
| 二度あることは三度ある。 | One thing leads to another. |
| 錬金術 | alchemy<br>錬金術師 alchemist |
| インターネットの巨大な可能性を利用する | harness the vast potential of the Internet<br>harness には「馬具」「馬具をつける」の意味もあります。 |

| | |
|---|---|
| 慧眼(けいがん), 洞察力 | acumen<br>商才 business acumen |
| 洞察力のある, 明敏な | astúte |
| 先見の明のある人 | a man of vision |
| そのあとで私は啓示を受けた, ひらめいた。 | Then I had my euréka moment.<br>eurekaは, アルキメデスが王冠の金の純度を調べる方法を思いついたときに発した言葉で, ギリシア語で「わかった」の意味です。今はカリフォルニア州の標語にもなっています。 |

# part 15

# 社会・文化

①少子化
②出産奨励策
③単身赴任者
④老人パワー
⑤介護保険
⑥離婚の件数が横ばいになる
⑦抗菌グッズ
⑧キレる
⑨援助交際
⑩予選
⑪ＰＫ戦
これをあなたは英語でいえますか？

# ◆ 少子化問題

| | |
|---|---|
| 出生率 | birth rate |
| 出生率の低下 | ① decline of the birth rate<br>② declining birth rate |
| 一人の女性が一生に産む子供の数は減少傾向にある。 | The number of children a woman bears in her lifetime is on the decline. |
| 少子化 | ① low fertility  ② less children |
| 出産奨励策 | incentives for newborns<br>newborn は「新生児」のことです。 |
| 育児休暇制度 | child-care leave program |
| 託児所不足 | shortage of day-care centers |
| 無認可保育園 | nursery school without licence<br>保母 nursery school teacher |
| 単身赴任者 | ① business bachelor<br>② field office bachelor<br>単身赴任 ① commuter marriage<br>　　　　　② long-distance marriage |
| 未婚の母 | single mother |
| 母体保護法 | Mother's Body Protection Law |
| 女性人権擁護団体 | organization ádvocating women's rights<br>advocate は動詞で「擁護する，唱道する」という意味です。また名詞では「擁護者」の意味になります。 |

## ◆ 家族の問題

| | |
|---|---|
| 家庭内暴力 | domestic violence [DV]<br>暴力をふるわれた妻 battered wife |
| 家庭内離婚 | marriage without love<br>仮面夫婦 formal marriage |
| 離婚の件数が横ばいになる。 | Divorces level off. |
| 両親が離婚した子供はそうでない子供に比べて離婚する可能性が約3倍ある。 | Children of divorced parents are nearly three times likely to divorce than their counterparts of intact families.<br>「(可能性が)50％高い」なら 50 percent more likely (to) となります。intact は「そのままの」, counterpart は「対をなすもの」の意味です。 |
| 今は家族がバラバラになっている。 | Families are so fragmented. |
| 核家族 | nuclear family<br>子供を溺愛する親 doting parent |
| 夫婦別姓 | separate surnames for married couples |

## ◆ 高齢化社会

| | |
|---|---|
| 高齢化, 老化 | aging<br>高齢化社会 aging society |

| | |
|---|---|
| 老人問題 | geriatric problem<br>老人病 geriatrics |
| 老人パワー | gray power |
| 老人ホーム | nursery home<br>有料の pay |
| 介護保険 | nursing care system<br>在宅介護 home health care |
| ひとりで暮らす老人 | elderly [old] people living alone |
| 今日の長寿を考えると… | Given [Supposed] today's longer life spans... |
| 福祉で最低限の生活をする | subsist on welfare<br>subsist は「何とか生活していく」の意味です。 |
| シルバー人材センター | placement office for senior citizens [the elderly]<br>placement office は「職業安定所」のことでしたね。「日常会話編」でやりました。 |
| 弱者 | weakling<br>支える prop up |

## ◆若者の風俗, 問題

| | |
|---|---|
| だらしな系ファッション | slob fashion<br>slob は「無精者」の意味です。<br>だぶだぶのズボン baggy pants |

## part 15 ● 社会・文化

| | |
|---|---|
| ポケベル | ① pager【péidʒər】<br>page には,「(空港・ホテルなどで)人の呼び出しをする」という意味があります。<br>② beeper |
| 抗菌グッズ | anti-bacterial goods<br>菌 ① bacteria【bæktíəriə】<br>② germ |
| いたるところに見られる | ubíquitous |
| 広く行き渡った | ① prevalent ② pervasive<br>広く行き渡る ① prevail ② pervade |
| 人気に火がついた。 | Its popularity caught fire.<br>この流行はスーッと消えていくだろう。<br>This fad will fizzle.<br>fizzle は「尻すぼみになる」という意味です。 |
| キレる | ① burst [fly] into a rage<br>② lose self-control |
| 自由を妨げるもの,拘束服 | strait[straight]jacket<br>日本社会の窮屈さ<br>straitjacket of Japanese social convention |
| 束縛 | constraint<br>打ち砕く shatter |
| 住みにくい社会 | dystópia<br>反対はもちろん utópia「理想郷」です。 |
| 物質的社会 | materialistic society |

| | |
|---|---|
| 摂食障害 | eating disorders |
| 援助交際 | juvenile prostitution<br>風俗産業 sex-related industry<br>誰とでも見さかいなく性交する promiscuous |

# ◆ オウム

| | |
|---|---|
| オウム真理教 | ① Aum Shinrikyo cult<br>② Aum Supreme Truth |
| カルト集団, カルト宗教 | cult<br>カルト宗教の信者 cultist<br>教団幹部 cult official(s) |
| オウム真理教の進出を防ぐ | stymie Aum settlement<br>stymie は「防ぐ, 妨害する」の意味で, stymie my career なら「私のキャリアを妨げる」という意味になります。 |
| 地下鉄サリン事件 | sarin attack in the subway (system)<br>神経ガス nerve gas |
| 12人を殺害し, 5千人以上の被害者を出した… | killing 12 people and sickening more than 5,000 |
| 砒素 | ársenic |
| 慰霊碑 | memorial<br>慰霊祭 memorial service<br>記念碑 monument |

# ◆サッカー人気

| | |
|---|---|
| 予選 | ① elimination(s)<br>② elimination match(es)<br>eliminate は「除外する，脱落させる」の意味です。 |
| 決勝(戦) | finals<br>しばしば複数で使います。<br>準決勝(戦) semi-finals |
| 前回の優勝者 | defending champion |
| ロスタイム | injury time |
| ＰＫ戦 | shootout |
| ヘッディング | ① header ② heading |
| 神技 | consummate【kənsʌ́mət】skill |
| 自殺点 | own goal |
| サッカーくじ | soccer lottery |
| フーリガン | hooligan |
| ジャージを脱ぎ捨てる | jerk his jersey off |
| 筋肉強化練習 | isometric exercises<br>isometric は【àisəmétrik】と発音します。 |
| ドーピング | doping<br>利尿剤 diuretic【dàiərétik】 |

## ◆映画

| | |
|---|---|
| 世界の恋人, 憧れの人 | heartthrob 【hάːrtθrὰb】<br>きらびやかな有名人, 名士 glitteráti<br>きらびやかな生活 glittery life |
| 子供たちをうっとりさせる | mesmerize kids |
| 興行主 | ① promoter ② impresário<br>impresario には「監督, 指揮者」の意味もあります。 |
| スーパースターを確保する | snatch [nab] a superstar |
| 上映する | screen<br>上映 screening<br>100万ドルを稼ぎ出した。<br>The film pulled [took] in a million dollars. |
| 映画の脚本 | screenplay |
| (俳優に向かって)幸運を祈るよ。 | Break a leg.<br>これは決まり文句です。 |
| 前編 | prequel<br>後編 sequel |
| 月並みな映画 | run-of-the-mill film<br>「月並みな」は banal を使うこともできます。 |
| お粗末な映画 | lousy film<br>気のぬけた vapid 【vǽpid】 |

| | |
|---|---|
| 超豪華な | spectácular |
| 酷評する | ① maul ② lambast |
| | こきおろす ① slam ② pan |
| 切って捨てる | dismiss the film |
| | 脚本がお粗末なB級映画として |
| | as a poorly written B movie |
| 汚い言葉 | foul language |
| | 映画については,「日常会話編（下）」のpart 20でもやりましたのでぜひ参考にしてください。 |
| 大河小説,武勇伝 | saga |
| 秘密試写会 | sneak preview |
| メディアを回避する | skirt the media |

## ◆叙勲, 文化遺産

| | |
|---|---|
| 叙勲制度 | honoring program |
| 勲章 | ① order ② decoration ③ medal |
| | ①は主に勲位を表します。③はコインの勲章のことです。 |
| 文化勲章 | Order of Cultural Merit |
| 勲章を授ける | ① confer ② award |
| 受勲者,受賞者 | laureate |
| | ノーベル賞受賞者 Nobel laureate |

| | |
|---|---|
| 名人 | **virtuoso**【vɜ̀ːrtʃuóusou】 |
| 人間国宝 | **living national treasure**<br>「国宝」や「文化財」については「日常会話編（下）」でもやりました。 |
| 文化遺産 | **cultural heritage** |
| 歴史的建造物の修復 | **restoration of historical assets** |

# part 16

# 野 球

さあ,どうでしょう。だいぶニュース,ビジネス英語が飲みこめたでしょうか。ここで少し息抜きをかねて,野球の英語を勉強してみてください。

①オープン戦
②対戦する
③黒星を喫する
④楽勝する
⑤1回裏に
⑥サイドスロー
⑦二桁勝利投手
⑧見送りの三振をする
これをあなたは英語でいえますか？

## ◆球場

| | |
|---|---|
| (野)球場 | ① ballpark ② stadium<br>stadium は本来は「競技場」の意味です。 |
| グラウンド, 球場 | (baseball) field |
| 人工芝 | ① artificial turf ② Astroturf<br>Astroturf はもとは商標名です。 |
| ファウルグラウンド | ① foul territory ② foul ground<br>フェアグラウンド fair territory |
| バックネット | backstop<br>backnet とはいいません。 |
| ネット裏の席 | ground stand<br>ここでの stand は「観覧席」を指します。<br>**ネット裏の席がとれた。**<br>**I got a seat in the ground stand.** |
| 内野席 | infield stand<br>外野席 ① outfield stand<br>　　　 ② bleachers<br>bleachers は「(屋根のない)観覧席」の意味です。 |

## ◆シーズン

| | |
|---|---|
| シーズンオフ | off-season |
| 春季キャンプ | spring training |

*part 16* ● 野球

| | |
|---|---|
| オープン戦 | exhibition game |
| ナイター | night game |
| 中断 | suspension<br>中断した suspended |
| 八百長試合 | put-up game |
| 没収試合 | forfeit 【fɔ́ːrfit】<br>放棄試合 forfeited game |

## ◆勝負, 順位

| | |
|---|---|
| チームを率いる | guide the team<br>采配を振る, 支配する call the shots |
| 巨人が阪神と対戦する。 | The Giants face [play] the Tigers. |
| ヤンキーズに勝つ | win against the Yankees<br>破る beat [defeat] the Yankees |
| (巨人を)下す | down (the Giants)<br>打ち破る clobber |
| 連勝 | winning streak<br>三連勝 three straight wins |
| わけなく | hands down |
| 巨人が阪神に負けた。 | The Giants lost to the Tigers.<br>4対3で (by the score of) four to three |
| 黒星を喫する | suffer a loss |

169

| | |
|---|---|
| 引き分け | ① tie (game) ② draw (game) <br> 同点 tie |
| せり勝つ | edge (out) |
| ヤンキースに楽勝する | ① romp away with the Yankees <br> ② romp home to the Yankees <br> ③ romp past the Yankees |
| 逆転する | ① come from behind <br> ② turn the tables [tide] <br> ③ turn face about |
| 形勢が逆転した。 | The tables are turned. |
| 逆転勝ち | come-from-behind victory <br> 逆転ホームラン <br> come-from-behind home run |
| 彼のホームランが試合の流れを変えた。 | His home run turned the tide in the game. |
| もつれ試合 | knotted game |
| 回 | ① inning ② frame |
| 1回表に | in the top of the first inning <br> 1回裏に <br> in the bottom of the first inning |
| 優勝する | ① win the pennant <br> ② win the championship |
| 王座を明け渡す, 手放す | relinquish their reign <br> reignは「統治」のことです。 |
| 最下位 | cellar <br> cellarは本来は「地下, (ワイン) セラー」 |

の意味です。

ヤンキースは最下位に終わった。
The Yankees ended up in the cellar.

| | |
|---|---|
| 首位, 1位 | ① first place ② top slot |
| 首位チーム | front-runner<br>首位の front-running |
| 首位になる | move into first place<br>首位に返り咲く<br>① move back into first place<br>② return to first place<br>1位とか2位には the がつきません。 |
| 首位を守る | hold top place |
| 首位から引きずり下ろす | blast the Giants out of top slot |
| (巨人を順位で)上回る | better (the Giants) |
| 優勝争いが激しくなる。 | The pennant race is really heating up. |

## コラム　選手・監督

### 選手

| | |
|---|---|
| ①投手 | (1) pitcher |
| | (2) hurler |
| | hurlは「強く投げる」という意味です。 |
| ②捕手 | catcher |
| ③一塁手 | first baseman |
| | 「塁手」にはbasemanのかわりにsackerを使うこともあります。 |
| ④二塁手 | second baseman |
| ⑤三塁手 | third baseman |
| ⑥ショート | shortstop |
| ⑦レフト | left fielder |
| ⑧センター | center fielder |
| ⑨ライト | right fielder |
| ⑩内野手 | infielder |
| ⑪外野手 | outfielder |
| ⑫打者 | (1) batter |
| | (2) hitter |
| | (3) batsman |
| ⑬代打 | pinch hitter |
| ⑭代走 | pinch runner |
| ⑮控え選手 | backup |
| ⑯交替要員 | substitute |

## 監督, その他

① 監督 　　　　　　　(field) manager
　　　　　　　　　　　field をつけるのは,「総監督」
　　　　　　　　　　　general manager と区別する必
　　　　　　　　　　　要のあるときです。
② コーチ　　　　　　coach
③ 球審　　　　　　　plate umpire
④ 塁審　　　　　　　base umpire
⑤ 主審　　　　　　　(1) chief umpire
　　　　　　　　　　　(2) umpire-in-chief
⑥ 線審　　　　　　　line judge
⑦ マネージャー　　　team's caretaker
⑧ チームの応援団長　holler guy
　　　　　　　　　　　holler は「大声を上げる」という
　　　　　　　　　　　意味です。
⑨ 解説者　　　　　　(1) commentator
　　　　　　　　　　　(2) analyst

# ◆投手陣

| | |
|---|---|
| 投手陣 | pitching staff |
| 右投手 | ① right-hander<br>② right-handed pitcher |
| 左投手 | ① left-hander<br>② left-handed pitcher<br>③ lefty ④ southpaw<br>southpaw の paw とは「(動物の) 足, (人の) 手」のことで, 昔シカゴの球場では, 左腕が南側を指していたことから, この言葉が生まれたとする説と, 南部出身者に左ききの投手が多かったからとする説があります。 |
| サイドスロー(投手), 横手投げ投手 | sidearmed pitcher |
| 下手投げ投手 | ① underarmed pitcher<br>② underhanded pitcher |
| オーバースロー(投手) | overhanded pitcher |
| エース | ace (pitcher) |
| 先発投手 | ① starter ② starting pitcher |
| リリーフ投手 | ① reliever ② relief pitcher<br>ワンポイントリリーフ spot reliever |
| リリーフ投手にマウンドを譲った。 | He gave way to the reliever.<br>give way to で「~に (道を) 譲る」の意味です。 |

| | |
|---|---|
| すぐピッチャーを替える監督［コーチ］ | quick hook |
| 中継ぎ投手 | middle-reliever<br>中継ぎ投手陣 middle-relief corps<br>corps は単数のときは【kɔːr】，複数のときは【kɔːrz】「コーズ」と発音することに注意してください。もともとは軍隊の「隊」のことです。<br>抑えの切り札の前に出てくる中継ぎ投手のことを，別に **set-upper** と呼ぶこともあります。 |
| 抑えの投手，切り札 | ① **closer** ② **stopper**<br>火消し **fireman**<br>fireman は一般用語では「消防士」のことです。 |
| 9回に登板する | work the ninth (inning) |
| 18個目のセーブ（ポイント）をあげる | pick up [earn] his 18th save |
| バッティング投手 | batting-practice pitcher |

## ◆ 勝利投手，敗戦投手

| | |
|---|---|
| 勝利投手 | winning pitcher<br>敗戦投手 losing pitcher |
| 勝利投手になった。 | ① He got [gained] credit for the win.<br>② The win [victory] went to him. |

| | |
|---|---|
| 7勝目をあげる | pick up [earn, notch] his 7th win |
| 二桁勝利投手 | double-figure winner<br>最多勝投手　winningest pitcher |
| 敗戦投手になった。 | ① He was charged with the loss.<br>② The loss was charged to him.<br>③ The loss went to him. |
| 完投(試合) | complete game<br>完投する　① pitch a complete game<br>　　　　　② go the distance |
| 完封 | shutout<br>完封する　① shut out　② blank |
| 1対0で完封した。 | He blanked the Tigers 1-0.<br>1-0 は one to zero といいます。 |
| 横浜を0点に抑える | hold Yokohama scoreless |
| 完全試合 | perfect game<br>完全試合を達成する<br>pitch a perfect game |
| ノーヒットノーラン | ① no-hitter　② no-hit-no-run<br>②の run は「得点」のことです。 |

## ◆投球

| | |
|---|---|
| 速球, 直球 | fastball<br>「直球」は正しくは straight ball ですが, 今この言葉はあまり使われません。 |

*part 16* ● 野 球

| | |
|---|---|
| 速球投手 | ① fastballer ② fastball pitcher |
| 剛速球 | ① fireball ② smoke<br>剛速球投手 fireballer |
| 変化球 | breaking ball |
| カーブ | ① curve ball ② hook<br>スライダー slider |
| シュート, スクリューボール | screwball<br>shoot とはいいません。バスケットボールの「シュート」は shot といいます。 |
| フォークボール | forkball<br>この fork は「ナイフとフォーク」のフォークのことで, このボールを投げるときの指の形から生まれた表現です。 |
| ナックルボール | knuckleball<br>knuckle は「指の関節」のことです。 |
| ストライク | strike<br>空振りのストライク swinging strike<br>判定のストライク called strike |
| ファール | foul<br>ファールチップ foul tip |

## ◆三振

| | |
|---|---|
| 三振 | strikeout<br>三球三振 strikeout on three pitches |
| 三振に打ちとる | ① strike out（the batter） ② fan |

| | |
|---|---|
| | 空振りの三振に打ちとる whiff |
| 三振する | ① strike out<br>② go down |
| 空振りの三振をする | strike out swinging |
| 見送り[見逃し]の三振をする | ① strike out taking a pitch<br>② strike out looking<br>見送る,見逃す take a pitch |
| 三振の数がリーグ一だ。 | He leads the league in strikeouts. |
| 決め球,ウィニングショット | ① strikeout pitch ② out pitch<br>winning shot とはいわないので注意してください。 |

# ◆コース,カウント

| | |
|---|---|
| 内角高目,インハイ | ① high and inside ② up and in<br>「インコース」「アウトコース」とはいわないので注意してください。また英語では日本語とは逆に,高さを先にいい,コースを後からいいます。<br>内角低目,インロー<br>① low and inside ② down and in |
| 外角高目 | ① high and outside ② up and away<br>外角低目 ① low and outside<br>② down and away |
| 真ん中 | middle |

## part 16 ● 野 球

| | |
|---|---|
| 内角へ投げる | **jam the batter**<br>jam は「無理に押し込む，（場所を）ふさぐ」の意味です。<br>⇔ **外角いっぱいに投げる nibble** |
| コーナーをつく | ① **paint the corner(s)**<br>② **hit the corner(s)** |
| 内角へ食い込む | **on the fists** |
| コントロールの抜群にいいピッチャー | **spot pitcher**<br>spot は「地点，箇所」の意味です。狙った所を外さないピッチャー，というニュアンスですね。 |
| 球が甘い | **fat**<br>甘い球 **fat pitch** |
| ホームランボール | **gopher ball**<br>ホームランボールを投げる **gopher** |
| カウント | **count** |
| ツー・スリー | **three (balls) and two (strikes)**<br>これも日本とは逆に，英語では「ボール」のほうから先に数えます。 |
| 打者をツー・ワンと追い込んだ。 | **He has put the batter in the hole with one ball and two strikes.** |
| 追い込まれた。 | **He was put in the hole.**<br>**I have two strikes against me.**「不利な立場にある，追い込まれた」ともいいます。どちらも野球に限らず，一般表現としても使います。 |

| | |
|---|---|
| 打ちとる | outpitch |
| 不利になる。 | He is behind. |

# ◆フォアボール

| | |
|---|---|
| フォアボール, 四球 | ① walk ② base on balls<br>four balls とはいわないので注意してください。 |
| 歩かせる | walk the hitter |
| 四球を与える | give him a base on balls<br>四球を出す issue a walk |
| 歩く | walk<br>四球を選ぶ draw a walk<br>draw は「引き寄せる, 招く」の意味です。 |
| フルカウントから | on a full count |
| ノーコンだ。 | ① He lacks (of) control.<br>② He has no control. |
| コントロールが悪い[良い]。 | He has a bad [good] control. |
| 敬遠のフォアボール | intentional walk<br>intentional は「故意の」という意味です。 |
| 敬遠する | ① walk him intentionally<br>② give him a base on balls intentionally |
| 歩かされた。 | He was walked intentionally. |

| | |
|---|---|
| ストレートの四球 | walk on four straight pitches |
| 押し出しのフォアボール | ① bases-loaded walk<br>② merry-go-round |

## ◆死球, 調子

| | |
|---|---|
| デッドボール, 死球 | ① hit-by-pitch  ② hit by a pitch |
| 暴投 | ① wild pitch  ② overthrow<br>日本語の「オーバースロー投手, 上手投げ投手」のことは overhanded pitcher というのでしたね。 |
| パスボール | **passed ball**<br>pass ball ではありませんので注意してください。 |
| ウェストボール | ① waste pitch  ② garbage pitch |
| 胸の高さのボール | **letter high**<br>letter はユニフォームのチーム名を書いた文字のことです。 |
| ブラッシュボール | ① brushback  ② duster  ③ Gillet<br>Gillet はまさしく「カミソリ」の商標名です。 |
| ビーンボール | **bean ball**<br>故意の投球, 危険球  purpose pitch |
| 危ない球をよける | **bail out**<br>経済用語ではこれは「救済する」という意味になります。 |

| | |
|---|---|
| 球審は退場を命じた。 | The plate unpire ordered him off the field. |
| 牽制球を投げる | make a pick-off throw |
| 牽制でアウトにする, 刺す | pick off the runner<br>牽制でアウトになった。<br>He was picked off. |
| ベースに釘づけにする, リードを取らせない | hold the runner |
| ボーク(をする) | balk<br>この言葉は一般には, balk at で「〜をためらう」の意味で使います。 |
| サインに首を振る | shake off a sign<br>「(選手などの)サイン」なら autograph, 「(署名などの)サイン」なら signature です。 |
| 相手方の攻撃を終わらせる | retire the side |
| 自責点 | earned run<br>非自責点 unearned run |
| 防御率 | earned run average ［ERA］ |
| 3点を許す | allow［give up］three runs<br>6安打を許す allow six hits<br>散発6安打に抑える scatter six hits<br>3点を失う, 与える yield three runs |
| 調子が悪い[いい]。 | I'm in bad［good］condition.<br>絶好調だ。He is really on the roll. |

*part 16* ● 野球

| | |
|---|---|
| 自信満々 | full of confidence |
| 本調子を出す,本調子になる | hit his stride<br>stride は「歩幅」のことです。 |
| 調子が出てきた。 | I've got into the swing of things. |
| その調子だ。 | Keep it up. |
| 緊張して堅くなる | choke up |

## ◆打者,打撃

| | |
|---|---|
| トップバッター,先頭打者 | lead off (man, hitter)<br>各イニングの先頭打者の意味もあります。top batter とはいわないので注意してください。 |
| 打順 | batting order |
| 上位打線 | top of the order<br>⇔ 下位打線 bottom of the order |
| 打率 | batting average |
| 首位打者 | leading hitter<br>三冠王 Triple Crown |
| 4番打者 | cleanup batter<br>日本ではクリーンアップバッターは,3～5番までの打者のことをいいますが,英語では,cleanup batter といえば「4番打者」のことです。走者を「一掃する」clean up というところから来ています。 |

183

| | |
|---|---|
| 指名打者 | designated hitter |
| 強打者 | ① slugger ② power hitter ③ heavy striker |
| 強打する | ① slug ② smash ③ slam ④ blast<br>この他にも lash, crush, belt などいろいろな言葉が使えます。 |
| ホームランバッター | ① home run slugger<br>② home run producer |
| 長距離打者 | longball hitter |
| 勝負強い打者 | clutch hitter<br>clutch には「(試合の) 最高の山場」の意味もあります。この clutch は車の「クラッチ」と同じ言葉です。 |
| 選球眼のいい打者 | selective hitter<br>選球眼 batting eye |
| 狙い打ちする打者 | guess hitter<br>読みが当たった。I guessed it right. |
| 野球選手には頭が必要だ。 | Baseball players need smarts [brains].<br>この smarts は複数形で,「抜け目のなさ, 明敏さ」などの意味になります。 |
| 広角に打ち分ける打者 | spray hitter |
| 流し打ちのヒット | ① opposite-field hit ② off-field hit<br>流し打ち opposite-field hitting |
| 流し打つ | hit a ball into the opposite field |

| | |
|---|---|
| 引っぱり専門の打者 | pull hitter |
| 巧打者 | connect hitter<br>うまく合わせる connect<br>この connect は **connect for a home run**「ホームランを打つ」というようにも使います。 |

## ◆打席に入って

| | |
|---|---|
| 打席 | batter's box<br>batter box ではありません。 |
| 三打席目に | in his third at bat<br>(right) off the bat といえば,一般用語で,「ただちに,ためらうことなく」の意味になります。 |
| 走者二塁で打席に立つ。 | He is at bat with a man [runner] on second. |
| ランナー一,三塁 | runners at the corners<br>ランナーなし no men on (bases) |
| お膳立ては整いました。 | The table is set. |
| 打席に入る | step up to the plate |
| ネクストバッターズサークル | on-deck (batter's) circle<br>次の打者は松井です。<br>Matsui is on deck. |

| | |
|---|---|
| バットを短めに持つ | **choke up the bat**<br>この表現はテニスなどのラケットやゴルフのクラブを短めに持つときにも使えます。<br>ラケットを短めに持つ<br>**choke up the（tennis）racket**<br>クラブを短めに持つ<br>**choke up the（golf）club** |
| ボールをたたきつける | **chop**<br>たたきつけられたボール **chopper** |
| 力いっぱい振る | **swing from the heels** |
| ファウルに逃れる | **guard [protect] the plate** |
| ボールに当てる | **get hold of the ball** |
| バットの芯 | **sweet spot** |
| 速球を打ち返す | **turn around a fastball** |
| 高目のボールを狙う | **wait for a high（ball）** |
| ヒットエンドラン | **run and hit**<br>これも日本とは語順が逆になります。 |
| スクイズ(する) | **squeeze** |
| バント(する) | **bunt**<br>ドラッグバント **drag bunt** |
| 残塁させる | ① strand ② leave |
| 2者残塁です。 | ① **They stranded two runners.**<br>② **Two runners were left on bases.** |

*part 16* ● 野 球

# ◆さまざまな打球

| | |
|---|---|
| フライ | fly (ball)<br>フライを打ち上げる ① hit a fly ② fly |
| サードフライ | fly ball to third<br>サードへフライを打ち上げた。<br>He flied to third. |
| センターフライでアウトになった。 | He hit a fly ball out to center field. |
| 平凡なフライ | routine fly |
| 打ち上げました！ | In the air! |
| イージーフライ | easy to catch |
| ポップフライ,小飛球 | ① pop fly ② pop-up<br>ポップフライを打ち上げる pop up |
| 内野フライ | infield fly |
| 犠牲フライ | sacrifice fly<br>犠牲バント sacrifice bunt |
| ファウルフライ | foul fly |
| ファウルになりそうです。 | ① The ball is likely to be to the foul territory.<br>② The ball seems to be to the foul territory. |
| ライナー | ① liner ② (line) drive ③ darter<br>弾丸ライナー bullet |
| ライナーを打つ | ① hit a liner ② line a single<br>③ rifle a single |

187

| | |
|---|---|
| いい当たりをする | **hit a drive** |
| 三塁手を動けなくする | **handcuff the third baseman**<br>handcuff は「手錠」「手錠をかける」の意味です。 |
| ゴロ | ① **grounder** ② **ground ball**<br>三塁ゴロ **grounder to third** |
| ゴロを打つ | **ground**<br>三塁ゴロを打った。<br>**He grounded to third.**<br>三塁ゴロを打ってアウトになった。<br>**He grounded out to third.** |
| ピッチャーゴロ | ① **grounder to the pitcher**<br>② **comebacker**<br>投手が投げたボールがまた投手に戻ってくるところから，②の表現が生まれました。 |
| 強いゴロ | **hard grounder**<br>⇔ 弱いゴロ **weak grounder** |
| 外野に達するゴロのヒット | ① **daisy [grass] clipper**<br>② **daisy [grass] cutter**<br>daisy は「ヒナギク」のことですね。 |
| イレギュラーバウンド | ① **bad bounce** ② **bad hop**<br>hop は「ぴょんとはねる（こと）」という意味です。<br>イレギュラーバウンドする<br>**take a bad hop** |

## part 16 ● 野球

| | |
|---|---|
| むずかしいいやなゴロ | nasty ground ball |
| ゴロをはじく | boot a grounder |

# ◆ヒット

| | |
|---|---|
| シングルヒット | single (hit) |
| ポテンヒット | ① Texas leaguer's hit<br>② Texas leaguer<br>昔テキサスリーグ・テレドの選手アート・サンデーがよくこのヒットを打ったことから生まれた言葉です。<br>③ blooper |
| ポテンヒットを打つ | ① bloop ② hit a Texas leaguer |
| 内野安打 | ① infield hit ② beatout |
| 内野ゴロを足でヒットにする | beat out |
| かろうじてのヒット | scratch hit |
| 内野手のあいだを抜けるヒット | betweener |
| タイムリーヒット | ① run-scoring hit ② timely hit |
| 2点タイムリー | two-run-scoring hit |
| 安打を集中する | bunch<br>bunch は本来は「房, 束 (にする)」などの意味です。 |

| | |
|---|---|
| 先発投手に襲いかかる, 早目に打ち崩す | jump all over the starter |
| 15本のヒットを打つ | rap out 15 hits<br>rap out は「たたき出す」という感じです。 |
| 巨人打線が爆発して13本のヒットを打った。 | The Giants exploded for 13 hits. |
| 乱打戦 | slugfest |

## ◆長打

| | |
|---|---|
| 長打, ロングヒット | ① extra-base hit ② long hit |
| 長打する | ① slug ② swat ③ clout ④ blast |
| 長打率 | slugging average |
| 二塁打 | ① two-base（hit）② double<br>③ two-bagger<br>bag はベースのことです。 |
| エンタイトルツーベース | ground-rule double<br>ゆうゆうの二塁打 stand-up double |
| 三塁打 | ① three-base（hit）② triple<br>③ three-bagger |
| サイクルヒット | cycle<br>サイクルヒットを打つ<br>hit for the cycle |
| ライト線 | （down）the right field line |

| | |
|---|---|
| ベースライン | baseline<br>ファウルライン foul line |
| 三塁線 | third baseline<br>一塁線 first baseline |
| 右中間 | right-center (field)<br>左中間 left-center (field)<br>右中間，左中間を合わせて **alleys** とか **lanes** ということもあります。 |
| センター前 | in front of the center fielder |
| ライトオーバー | over the right fielder<br>over the right fielder's head ということもあります。<br>レフトオーバー<br>over the left fielder('s head) |

## ◆ホームラン

| | |
|---|---|
| ホームラン，本塁打 | ① homer ② home run ③ blast<br>ホームランは他に，**round tripper** とか **dinger, four-bagger** といった言い方もします。 |
| ランニングホームラン | inside-the-park homer |
| スリーラン | three-run homer<br>ソロホームラン solo homer |
| ホームランを打つ，放つ，かっとばす | ① hit a home run<br>② blast a home run |

|  |  |
|---|---|
|  | ③ rip a home run<br>①が「打つ」，②が「放つ」，③が「かっとばす」という感じです。他に「強打する」のところで覚えた belt などの言葉も使えます。<br>レフトスタンドにホームランを打ちこむ<br>hit a home run into the left stands |
| 満塁ホームラン | ① grand slam<br>② bases-loaded home run<br>③ home run with the bases loaded |
| サヨナラホームラン | game-ending home run<br>均衡を破るホームラン<br>tiebreaking home run |
| 通算本塁打 | career home runs |
| ホームランを放って阪神に広島戦での勝利をもたらした。 | ① He hit a home run to lift Hanshin to a victory over Hiroshima.<br>② He hit a home run to power Hanshin to win over Hiroshima. |

# ◆打点

|  |  |
|---|---|
| 打点 | run(s) batted in ［RBI］<br>RBI は ribby とも読みます。 |
| 勝利打点 | game-winning RBI |
| 3打点を上げた。 | ① He drove in three runs.<br>② He had three RBIs. |

*part 16* ◉ 野 球

| | |
|---|---|
| 決勝点 | game-winning run |
| 勝ち越し点 | go-ahead run |
| | 勝ち越しの go-ahead |
| リードして | ahead |

## ◆ 走塁

| | |
|---|---|
| ランナー | (base) runner |
| 走塁 | base running |
| 出塁する | get [go] to first base |
| 出塁率 | on-base percentage |
| | 高い出塁率 high on-base percentage |
| 二塁へ進塁する | advance to second |
| 俊足の選手 | speedster |
| | 足のある打者 leg hitter |
| 盗塁(する) | ① steal ② swipe |
| | 盗塁数 stolen bases [SB] |
| 二[三]塁へ盗塁した。 | He stole second [third]. |
| | ホームスチールする steal home |
| 二塁への盗塁に成功した。 | He made a steal to second. |
| | 盗塁に失敗した。 He failed to steal. |
| 一試合に3つ盗塁する | steal three bases in a single game |
| ヘッドスライディング | headfirst sliding |

193

| | |
|---|---|
| | 二塁へヘッドスライディングする<br>① slide head first into second<br>② dive into second |
| 一塁へ頭から滑り込んでセーフになった。 | He dived into first safely. |
| 満塁 | ① bases loaded  ② bases full<br>満塁にする  load bases |
| タッチアップする | tag up<br>タッチアップ  tagging up |
| サードコーチャー | third base coach<br>サードコーチャーを務める<br>serve as a third base coach |
| タッチアウトにする | tag out<br>ホームでタッチアウトになった。<br>He was tagged out at the plate.<br>単に「タッチする」だけなら，tag となります。野球用語では touch は「ベースを踏む」というときに，touch the base という形で使います。 |
| ベースを踏み損なう，踏み忘れる | ① miss touching the base<br>② forget to touch the base |
| タッチを避ける | avoid a tag |
| アウトにする | put him out |
| フォースアウトにする | force out<br>フォースアウト  force-out |
| 送球でアウトにする | nail |

| | |
|---|---|
| | 送球 peg |
| 三本間にはさまれた。 | He was trapped between third and home. |
| 挟殺する | run down<br>挟殺 rundown |
| ホームインする,(ホームに)生還する | ① come [reach] home ② come in<br>③ score ④ cross home [the plate] |
| 高橋のヒットで生還した。 | He scored on Takahashi's hit. |
| 無得点 | ① no run ② goose egg |

## ◆ 守備

| | |
|---|---|
| キャッチャーミット | catcher's mitt<br>ファーストミット<br>first baseman's glove |
| プロテクター | chest protector |
| レガース | ① shin guards<br>② leg guards<br>日本語のレガースはこれが変化したものです。 |
| キャッチャーマスク | mask<br>膝パッド knee pad |
| すべり止め | cleat<br>cleats と複数になると「スパイクシューズ」の意味にもなります。 |

| | |
|---|---|
| ボールの縫い目 | seam |
| 守備 | ① defense<br>⇔ 攻撃 offense<br>② fielding<br>⇔ 打撃 batting |
| 一塁を守る | play first base<br>センターを守る play center field |
| 三塁 | hot corner |
| 堅実な守備の内野陣 | sure-handed infield |
| グラブさばき | glove work |
| 前進守備の | draw-in |
| ライン際を固める | guard the lines |
| ダブル[トリプル]プレー | double [triple] play<br>5-4-3のダブルプレー<br>around-the-horn double play |
| ダブルプレーをする | turn a double play<br>ダブルプレーを防ぐ<br>break up the double play |
| 捕球する | ① catch ② make a catch |
| いい守備を見せる | make a good play [catch] |
| ジャンピングキャッチ | ① jumping catch ② leaping catch |
| ダイビングキャッチ | diving catch |
| シングルキャッチ | one-handed catch |

## part 16 ● 野球

| | |
|---|---|
| | 素手でキャッチする<br>**make a barehanded catch** |
| ショートバウンド | **short hop**<br>うまく救い上げる **short-hop**<br>救い上げる **dig out** |
| 地面すれすれでの捕球 | **shoestring catch**<br>「靴ひものあたりの捕球」ということです。 |
| 一塁のベースカバーをする | **cover first base**<br>ベースカバー **covering a base** |
| バックホーム(する) | **throw to the plate** |
| バックホームが右へ逸れた。 | **The throw to the plate was right.**<br>「大きく逸れた」なら was way right とか was wide right となります。 |
| 強肩 | ① **strong arm** ② **powerful throw** |
| 中継プレー | **relay** |
| カットプレー | **cutoff play** |
| クッションボール | ① **carom**【kǽrəm】<br>もともとはビリアードの用語です。<br>② **one-cushion shot** |
| クッションボールを処理した。 | **He got the carom.**<br>クッションボールの処理を誤る<br>**fumble the carom** |

## ◆エラー

| | |
|---|---|
| エラーする | commit [make] an error<br>手痛いエラー costly error |
| ファンブルする | ① fumble ② bobble |
| ボールをつかみ損なった。 | He couldn't find the handle. |
| はじく | boot |
| トンネルする | ① let the grounder go through his legs<br>② allow the grounder to go through his legs |
| ボーンヘッド | bonehead(ed) play |
| 落球(する) | muff<br>取り損なう fail to catch (a ball) |
| ボールを落とす | drop the ball |
| ボールから目を離す | take his eyes off the ball |

## ◆練習

| | |
|---|---|
| 練習 | practice<br>トレーニング training |
| キャッチボール | catch<br>キャッチボールをする play catch |

## part 16 ● 野 球

| | |
|---|---|
| ノック | fungo 【fʌ́ŋgou】<br>ノックする hit fungoes<br>ノックバット fungo bat |
| シートノック,守備練習 | fielding practice |
| トスバッティング | pepper (game) |
| 打撃練習 | batting practice<br>「バッティング練習ではすばらしい当たりを連発するのに本番で打てない打者」のことを，one [two] o'clock hitter ということもあります。練習時間がだいたいそれくらいだからです。 |

〈下巻に続く〉

# 日本語索引

## あ

| | |
|---|---|
| ILO | 36 |
| アイコン | 152 |
| 相手方の攻撃を終わらせる | 182 |
| アウトにする | 194 |
| 赤字国債 | 134 |
| 赤字を見込む | 45 |
| 空地 | 25 |
| 悪意のある | 123 |
| 憧れの人 | 164 |
| 足元にも及ばない | 109 |
| 明日の百より今日の五十 | 113 |
| 当たった瞬間に | 78 |
| 頭から当たる | 78 |
| 新しい道の開拓者 | 150 |
| 圧政 | 97 |
| あっせんする人 | 141 |
| あっせん利得 | 141 |
| あっと言わせる | 116 |
| 圧力団体 | 140 |
| 当てる | 27 |
| 兄弟子 | 76 |
| 危ない球をよける | 181 |
| 甘んじて屈辱を受ける | 116 |
| アメリカ議会 | 128 |
| アメリカ国税庁 | 70 |
| 争う | 87 |
| 歩かされた | 180 |
| 歩かせる | 180 |
| 歩く | 180 |
| 合わせる | 114 |
| 安価な労働力 | 48 |
| アンケート（用紙） | 91 |
| 暗号解読 | 154 |
| 暗号化する | 154 |
| 暗号を解読する | 154 |
| 暗示 | 123 |
| 暗礁に乗り上げる | 31 |
| 安全ネットの必要性 | 64 |
| 安打を集中する | 189 |
| 安定化 | 22 |
| 安定化する | 22 |

## い

| | |
|---|---|
| いい当たりをする | 188 |
| イージーフライ | 187 |
| いい守備を見せる | 196 |
| 委員会 | 127 |
| 委員長 | 105 |
| 意外な授かり物 | 29 |
| 行き詰まり | 134 |
| 行き詰まる | 134 |
| 異議を唱える | 121 |
| 育児休暇制度 | 158 |
| 意見に反論する | 121 |
| 意見の分かれる問題 | 120 |
| 移行 | 100 |
| 異彩を放つ | 116 |
| 意志の堅い | 130 |
| いずれにしても | 38 |
| 遺族年金 | 37 |
| いたるところに見られる | 161 |
| 1位 | 171 |
| 一か八かの | 59 |
| 一時的下落 | 64 |
| 一時的な | 100 |
| 一時的要因 | 46 |
| 一日につき | 29 |
| 一年につき | 29 |
| 一年前に比べて | 46 |
| 一枚岩 | 106 |
| 一枚岩の | 106 |
| 一率課税 | 71 |
| 一塁のベースカバーをする | 197 |
| 一塁を守る | 196 |
| 1回裏に | 170 |
| 1回表に | 170 |
| 一括法案 | 129 |
| 一気に | 79 |
| 一極集中 | 145 |
| 一極に集中した | 145 |
| 一般会計 | 132 |
| 一般教書 | 129 |
| 一般教書演説をする | 129 |
| 一般大衆 | 102 |
| 一匹狼 | 116 |
| 違反 | 30 |
| 違反する | 40 |
| 違法行為 | 141 |
| 今はなき | 31 |
| 今やあなたは私の友なので… | 113 |
| イメージチェンジ | 89 |
| 医療費 | 38 |
| 慰霊祭 | 162 |
| 慰霊碑 | 162 |
| イレギュラーバウンド | 188 |
| イレギュラーバウンドする | 188 |
| 色あせさせる | 122 |
| 色あせた | 122 |
| インサイダー取引 | 65 |
| インターネット検索ページ | 153 |
| インターネットの巨大な可能性を利用する | 155 |
| 隠匿 | 142 |
| インフラの整備 | 19 |
| インフレ緩和 | 20 |

| | | | | | |
|---|---|---|---|---|---|
| インフレ対策 | 20 | **え** | | オウム真理教の進出を防 | |
| インフレと闘う | 20 | 映画の脚本 | 164 | ぐ | 162 |
| インフレを抑制する | 20 | 英語に堪能な | 153 | 横領 | 142 |
| **う** | | 英連邦 | 97 | 横領する | 142 |
| ウィニングショット | 178 | エース | 174 | （大）相撲 | 76 |
| ウェストボール | 181 | 液晶ディスプレイ | 152 | 大損する | 65 |
| 浮き彫りにした | 64 | 閲覧ソフト | 152 | 大関 | 77 |
| 受け入れ行 | 27 | エラーする | 198 | 大立者 | 109 |
| 受け皿銀行 | 32 | 選り好みの許されない選 | | 大手の | 59 |
| 打ち上げました | 187 | 択 | 115 | オーバースロー（投手） | |
| 打ち砕く | 161 | 延々たる攻撃演説 | 122 | | 174 |
| 打ちとる | 180 | エンゲル係数 | 19 | 大幅減税 | 72 |
| 打ち破る | 169 | 縁者びいき | 143 | オープン戦 | 169 |
| 右中間 | 191 | 援助交際 | 162 | 大見栄 | 116 |
| 内輪もめ | 108 | 演説の練習をする | 89 | 大物 | 109 |
| うなぎ昇りに上がる | 62 | 円相場 | 54 | お金をすくい取る | 24 |
| 右派 | 103,107 | エンタイトルツーベース | | 憶測が渦巻いている | 115 |
| うまく合わせる | 185 | | 190 | 送り出す | 79 |
| うまく工夫した機械装置 | | 円高 | 54 | 遅れをとっている | 16 |
| | 150 | 演壇で | 89 | 抑えの投手 | 175 |
| 生み出す | 63 | 円安 | 54 | 惜し気ない消費 | 19 |
| 右翼 | 103 | **お** | | 押し倒す | 79 |
| 裏書き | 32 | 追い込んだ | 179 | 押し出しのフォアボール | |
| 裏書きする | 32 | 追い払う | 117 | | 181 |
| 裏書き人 | 32 | オイルショック | 47 | 押し出す | 79 |
| 裏金 | 142 | 王位 | 96 | 汚職 | 141 |
| 裏切り | 117 | 王位継承 | 96 | おせっかい好きな | 108 |
| 裏切りかねない | 117 | 王位に就く | 96 | お膳立ては整いました | |
| 裏目に出る | 119 | 王位を継承する | 96 | | 185 |
| 裏をかく | 117 | 王位を継ぐ | 96 | 遅くとも3月までに | 17 |
| 売上税 | 70 | 応援演説 | 89 | 遅まきながらも | 56 |
| 売り注文 | 60 | 王権 | 96 | お粗末な映画 | 164 |
| ウルグアイ・ラウンド | 48 | 王国 | 96 | 弟弟子 | 76 |
| うるさい奴だ | 121 | 王座 | 96 | 落とし穴 | 118 |
| 上手 | 78 | 王座にのぼる | 96 | 思い上がった | 122 |
| 上手投げ | 79 | 王座を明け渡す | 170 | 思いきった措置 | 145 |
| 上回る | 171 | 欧州通貨統合 | 56 | 重荷を背負う | 119 |
| 運転資金 | 27 | 王朝 | 96 | 親方 | 76 |
| 運用資産 | 68 | 王の | 96 | お役所流 | 144 |
| | | オウム真理教 | 162 | およそ | 63 |

| 語句 | ページ |
|---|---|
| 折り合いをつける | 113 |
| 卸売物価 | 18 |
| 終値 | 61 |
| 穏健な | 103 |
| 温床 | 142 |
| 恩をあだで返した | 117 |

## か

| 語句 | ページ |
|---|---|
| カーブ | 177 |
| 回 | 170 |
| 害悪を及ぼす | 123 |
| 開会 | 128 |
| 開会する | 128 |
| 外角いっぱいに投げる | 179 |
| 外角高目 | 178 |
| 外角低目 | 178 |
| 外貨準備高 | 54 |
| 会期 | 127 |
| 懐疑論 | 115 |
| 会計検査院 | 132 |
| 会計年度 | 132 |
| 解雇 | 34 |
| 外交委員会 | 127 |
| 外国為替市場 | 54 |
| 解雇する | 34 |
| 解雇通知 | 35 |
| 介護保険 | 160 |
| 解散 | 128 |
| 解散する | 128 |
| 概算要求枠 | 133 |
| 会社更生手続きを申請する | 31 |
| 会社更生法 | 31 |
| 外需 | 18 |
| 回収可能な | 26 |
| 回収する | 26 |
| 回収不能な | 26 |
| 改正 | 58,85,132 |
| 改正する | 58,132 |
| 改造 | 25 |
| 海賊行為 | 151 |
| 海賊版 | 151 |
| 下位打線 | 183 |
| 外注 | 39 |
| 買い注文 | 60 |
| 改訂する | 132 |
| 回答者 | 91 |
| 介入 | 55 |
| 介入する | 55 |
| 解任 | 101 |
| 解任する | 101 |
| 開票 | 92 |
| 開票結果 | 92 |
| 開票結果を集計する | 92 |
| 開票する | 92 |
| 回復 | 18 |
| 買い戻し | 60 |
| 外野席 | 168 |
| 外野に達するゴロのヒット | 188 |
| 傀儡政権 | 98 |
| 下院 | 128 |
| 下院議員 | 129 |
| カウント | 179 |
| 価格をつり上げる | 18 |
| 輝きのない年 | 15 |
| 架空会社 | 30 |
| 格差 | 86 |
| 格差を2倍以内に抑える | 86 |
| 各種有価証券 | 68 |
| 革新 | 150 |
| 革新政党 | 105 |
| 革新的な | 150 |
| 隠す | 142 |
| 拡大する貿易黒字 | 45 |
| 格付け会社 | 27 |
| 確定給付契約 | 37 |
| 格闘する | 76 |
| 獲得する | 93 |
| 確保する | 94 |
| 額面 | 60 |
| 可決 | 130 |
| 可決する | 130 |
| 駆引の材料 | 36 |
| 駆引をする | 36,113 |
| 過去最高の黒字を記録する | 45 |
| 貸し方 | 26 |
| 貸し渋り | 27 |
| 貸し付け | 24 |
| 貸し付ける | 24 |
| 過剰設備 | 19 |
| 過剰融資 | 24 |
| 数で上回る | 108 |
| 課税 | 71 |
| 課税する | 71 |
| 稼ぎ出した | 164 |
| 過疎の | 86 |
| 偏りがある | 49 |
| 勝ち越し点 | 193 |
| 勝ち越しの | 193 |
| 火中の栗 | 119 |
| 画期的な出来事 | 119 |
| 活気に満ちた | 14 |
| ガット | 48 |
| カットプレー | 197 |
| 活発な | 14 |
| 合併 | 39 |
| 合弁企業 | 39 |
| 合併・買収(M&A) | 40 |
| 仮定する | 68 |
| 家庭内暴力 | 159 |
| 家庭内離婚 | 159 |
| 金がたっぷりある | 90 |
| 金をつかませる | 140 |
| 過半数 | 93 |
| 過半数すれすれ | 93 |
| 株価 | 61 |
| 株価収益率 | 63 |

# 日本語索引

| | | | | | |
|---|---|---|---|---|---|
| 株価の暴落 | 64 | 間接税 | 70 | 規制緩和 | 47 |
| 株（式） | 58 | 間接的に中傷する | 122 | 規制緩和する | 47 |
| 株式公開買付 | 40 | 完全試合 | 176 | 既成事実 | 135 |
| 株式市場 | 61 | 完全試合を達成する | 176 | 規制する | 46 |
| 株式仲介人 | 59 | 完投（試合） | 176 | 犠牲バント | 187 |
| 株式買入優先権 | 59 | 敢闘賞 | 81 | 犠牲フライ | 187 |
| 家父長制 | 108 | 完投する | 176 | 気勢を上げる集会 | 89 |
| 株主 | 58 | 堪忍袋の緒が切れた | 123 | 議席を失う | 93 |
| 株主総会 | 58 | 完封 | 176 | 議席を得る | 93 |
| 株主代表訴訟 | 58 | 完封する | 176 | 議席を100まで伸ばす | 94 |
| 株のもち合い | 60 | カンフル剤 | 17 | 毅然としている | 116 |
| 株を20%取得する | 60 | 官僚 | 144 | 競う | 87 |
| 過密の | 86 | 官僚主義 | 144 | 汚い言葉 | 165 |
| 神技 | 163 | 官僚的形式主義 | 144 | きっかけ | 114 |
| 仮面夫婦 | 159 | 緩和 | 47 | 切って捨てる | 165 |
| からいばり | 116 | **き** | | 規定 | 41 |
| 空騒ぎ | 108 | 議員 | 127 | 規定する | 40 |
| 空振りの三振をする | 178 | 議員同士の慣れ合い | 140 | 記念碑 | 162 |
| 空振りのストライク | 177 | 議会 | 127 | 技能賞 | 81 |
| 借り方 | 26 | 気が若い | 108 | 気のぬけた | 164 |
| カルト宗教 | 162 | 機関投資家 | 59 | 規範 | 119 |
| カルト宗教の信者 | 162 | 危機に瀕している | 117 | 基盤 | 88 |
| カルト集団 | 162 | 企業献金 | 89 | 厳しい試練を受ける | 31 |
| かろうじて | 130 | 企業支配 | 51 | 厳しく罰する | 143 |
| かろうじてのヒット | 189 | 企業年金 | 37 | 機敏な | 155 |
| 為替市場 | 54 | 企業の圧力にひるむ | 140 | 基本原理 | 150 |
| 為替相場メカニズム | 54 | 企業のイメージアップを | | 気前よくもてなす | 140 |
| 為替リスク | 54 | する | 41 | 決まり手 | 79 |
| かわりに就任する | 143 | （企業の）系列 | 49 | 気むずかしい | 108 |
| 考え込んだ | 120 | 企業の慈善活動 | 41 | 決めかねている | 115 |
| 甘言でつる | 113 | 棄権 | 91 | きめ出す | 79 |
| 甘言で手に入れる | 102 | 危険球 | 181 | 決め球 | 178 |
| 監査 | 29 | 棄権する | 91 | 逆ざや | 29 |
| 管財人 | 31 | 技術移転 | 151 | 逆転勝ち | 170 |
| 監査する | 29 | 技術的に熟達した | 153 | 逆転する | 170 |
| 幹事長 | 105 | 技術を移転する | 151 | 逆転ホームラン | 170 |
| 完勝 | 93 | 基準価格 | 18 | キャッチボール | 198 |
| 関税 | 46 | 議場 | 127 | キャッチボールをする | |
| 関税化 | 46 | 気色ばむ | 123 | | 198 |
| 関税障壁 | 46 | 規制 | 46 | キャッチャーマスク | 195 |

203

| | | | | | |
|---|---|---|---|---|---|
| キャッチャーミット | 195 | 行政改革 | 144 | 金権選挙 | 90 |
| 休会 | 128 | 行政指導 | 20 | 金権の | 106 |
| 休会する | 128 | 行政府 | 126 | 銀行が貸し渋る | 27 |
| 救済計画 | 32 | 行政命令 | 136 | 銀行業界 | 22 |
| 救済する | 32 | 強打者 | 184 | 均衡予算 | 133 |
| 救済措置 | 32 | 強打する | 184 | 僅差の勝利 | 93 |
| 吸収（合併） | 40 | 教団幹部 | 162 | 緊縮型になる | 134 |
| 吸収する | 40 | 協調介入に踏み切る | 56 | 緊縮 | 16 |
| 球場 | 168 | 強調する | 89 | 近親者 | 143 |
| 休場する | 80 | 協調利上げに踏み切る | 56 | 緊張して堅くなる | 183 |
| 急進的な | 103 | 共同体 | 39 | 筋肉強化練習 | 163 |
| 球審は退場を命じた | 182 | 今日の長寿を考えると | | 金脈 | 106 |
| 求心力 | 112 | | 160 | 金融改革 | 22 |
| 求人倍率 | 35 | 協力が不可欠だ | 113 | 金融緩和策 | 16 |
| 救世主 | 143 | 強力なグループ | 107 | 金融機関 | 23 |
| 急成長している | 154 | 共和国 | 96 | 金融業界 | 22 |
| 急先鋒 | 112 | 共和国への移行 | 96 | 金融システム | 22 |
| 急速に成長している市場 | | 共和党 | 85 | 金融システムの安定 | 22 |
| | 48 | 共和党員 | 85 | 金融自由化 | 22 |
| (旧)ソ連邦 | 97 | 極左(の) | 103 | 金融商品 | 23 |
| 急騰する | 62 | 巨人 | 109 | 金融派生商品 | 67 |
| 給与以外の福利厚生 | 39 | 巨人が阪神と対戦する | | 金融引締策 | 16 |
| 急落 | 23 | | 169 | 金融逼迫 | 27 |
| 急落する | 64 | 巨大企業 | 20 | **く** | |
| 驚異的な実績 | 109 | 拒否権(を発動する) | 131 | 草の根 | 88 |
| 教会の説教壇 | 89 | 清め | 77 | 下する | 80 |
| 強化する | 16 | 清めの塩をまく | 77 | 下す | 169 |
| 教義 | 104 | 清める | 77 | 口先介入 | 56 |
| 供給 | 18 | きらびやかな生活 | 164 | 口を濁した | 40 |
| 供給過剰 | 18 | きらびやかな有名人，名 | | クッションボール | 197 |
| 強肩 | 197 | 士 | 164 | 屈服する | 117 |
| 強硬に国会を通す | 130 | 切り上げ | 56 | 駆動装置 | 152 |
| 強硬派 | 104 | 切り下げ | 56 | 曇らせる | 122 |
| 挟殺 | 195 | 切り札 | 175 | グラウンド | 168 |
| 挟殺する | 195 | キレる | 161 | グラブさばき | 196 |
| 共産主義 | 98 | 記録する | 35 | クラブを短めに持つ | 186 |
| 共産主義者 | 98 | 岐路に立っている | 117 | クリックする | 152 |
| 共産党 | 105 | 疑惑 | 141 | クリントン政権 | 100 |
| 行司 | 77 | 菌 | 161 | 狂わせる | 131 |
| 行政 | 126 | 金権政治 | 106 | 黒星を喫する | 169 |

| | | | | | |
|---|---|---|---|---|---|
| 区割り | 86 | 経常赤字 | 28,45 | 見解 | 104 |
| 区割りをする | 86 | 経常黒字 | 45 | 減価償却 | 72 |
| 軍事政権 | 97 | 経常収支 | 45 | 元気いっぱいの | 108 |
| 君主 | 96 | 継承推定相続人 | 96 | 県議会 | 128 |
| 群集心理 | 106 | 経常利益 | 28 | 元気のいい | 155 |
| 君主国 | 96 | 啓示を受けた | 156 | 献金 | 89 |
| 君主制 | 96 | 形勢が逆転した | 170 | 献金する | 89 |
| 勲章 | 165 | 経団連 | 51 | 権限委譲 | 145 |
| 勲章を授ける | 165 | 経費 | 38 | 権限を委譲する | 145 |
| **け** | | 経費削減 | 38 | 検査 | 29 |
| 敬意を表して | 100 | 経費を抑える | 38 | 原材料 | 47 |
| 敬遠する | 180 | 経費を削減する | 38 | 検査する | 29 |
| 敬遠のフォアボール | 180 | 経費を節約する | 38 | 減資 | 67 |
| 警戒して | 66 | 軽蔑的な | 123 | 減資する | 67 |
| 計画経済 | 44 | 契約不履行 | 40 | 現実的なビジネス | 154 |
| 慧眼 | 156 | ケガをしやすい | 80 | 堅実な守備の内野陣 | 196 |
| 景気 | 14 | 化粧まわし | 76 | 元首 | 98 |
| 景気回復 | 17 | 結果として生じる | 16 | 減少傾向にある | 158 |
| 景気が回復しつつある | 17 | (結果は)まだわからない | | 現状を維持する | 16 |
| 景気後退 | 15 | | 92 | 現職の | 87 |
| 景気循環 | 14 | 決議 | 130 | 減税 | 72 |
| 景気上昇 | 17 | 決起集会 | 89 | 牽制球を投げる | 182 |
| 景気対策を講ずる | 17 | 決議する | 130 | 牽制でアウトにする, 刺 | |
| 景気停滞 | 15 | 決算 | 29 | す | 182 |
| 景気低迷 | 15 | 決選投票 | 93 | 減税要求 | 72 |
| 景気低迷下のインフレ | 20 | 決勝(戦) | 163 | 健全化する | 143 |
| 景気動向指数 | 14 | 決勝点 | 193 | 源泉課税 | 71 |
| 景気を刺激する | 17 | 決定を覆す | 131 | 健全性 | 26 |
| 景気をテコ入れする | 17 | 欠点のない | 109 | 源泉徴収(税) | 71 |
| 経済が加熱しすぎる危険 | | 結論に達する | 135 | 健全な | 26 |
| がある | 14 | 懸念 | 121 | 憲法改正 | 132 |
| 経済危機 | 15 | 懸念を抱いている | 121 | 原理主義 | 99 |
| 経済成長 | 17 | 懸念を表明する | 121 | 原理主義者 | 99 |
| 経済成長を維持する | 17 | 下落 | 54 | 権力[職権]の乱用 | 142 |
| 経済団体連合会 | 51 | 下落する | 64 | 権力闘争 | 112 |
| 経済的混乱 | 15 | 下落する | 54 | 権力にしがみつく | 110 |
| 経済同友会 | 51 | 懸案(事項) | 131 | 元老 | 108 |
| 経済白書 | 14 | 懸案の | 131 | 言論の自由 | 97 |
| 経済報告 | 129 | 減益 | 28 | **こ** | |
| 経済摩擦 | 46 | 喧嘩 | 121 | 故意の投球 | 181 |

| | | | | | |
|---|---|---|---|---|---|
| 幸運を祈るよ | 164 | 公認会計士 | 70 | 互恵 | 44 |
| 公開入札 | 50 | 広範囲の提携 | 39 | 互恵的貿易 | 44 |
| 広角に打ち分ける打者 | 184 | 公布 | 136 | こけおどし | 116 |
| 高級化 | 25 | 高付加価値製品 | 47 | 後光 | 109 |
| 恒久減税 | 72 | 公布する | 136 | 五十歩百歩だ | 123 |
| 好況 | 14 | 後編 | 164 | 個人需要 | 18 |
| 公共事業 | 19 | 合弁事業 | 39 | 個人消費 | 18 |
| 興行主 | 164 | 合法化する | 136 | 個人消費の落ち込み | 18 |
| 公共投資 | 19 | 候補者 | 87 | 国歌 | 98 |
| 抗菌グッズ | 161 | 候補者名簿 | 88 | 国会 | 126 |
| 好景気(になる) | 14 | 公明正大な | 143 | 国会議員 | 126 |
| 攻撃 | 196 | 公約 | 89 | 国会対策委員長 | 106 |
| 交際費 | 38 | 公約する | 89 | 国家主義 | 99 |
| 好材料 | 65 | 合理化 | 39 | 国家主義者 | 99 |
| 好材料は(相場に)織り込まれている | 66 | 工場を閉鎖する | 39 | 国家予算 | 132 |
| | | 合理化する | 39 | 国旗 | 98 |
| 公示価格 | 50 | 交流 | 152 | ご都合主義 | 123 |
| 公式な発表 | 136 | 綱領 | 104 | 固定資産税 | 70 |
| 工場を閉鎖する | 39 | 高齢化 | 159 | 固定相場制 | 54 |
| 公職から退ける | 143 | 高齢化社会 | 159 | 固定費 | 38 |
| 公職選挙法 | 85 | 口論 | 121 | 言葉を濁す | 40 |
| 高所得者層 | 72 | 口論する | 121 | 子供たちをうっとりさせる | 164 |
| 公正取引委員会 | 50 | 越える | 24 | | |
| 厚生年金 | 37 | コーナーをつく | 179 | 子供を溺愛する親 | 159 |
| 公然と非難する | 122 | こきおろす | 165 | このままでいく | 16 |
| 公然の | 142 | 小切手 | 32 | 小幅な動きをする | 55 |
| 構造的要因 | 46 | 国営企業 | 20 | 戸別訪問 | 88 |
| 構造不況 | 15 | 国際決済銀行 | 23 | 小回りのきく | 155 |
| 拘束服 | 161 | 国際的な役割を果たす | 49 | 込み入った | 120 |
| 剛速球 | 177 | 国際労働機関 | 36 | 小結 | 78 |
| 剛速球投手 | 177 | 国税庁 | 70 | コメ市場の部分開放 | 48 |
| 巧打者 | 185 | 国勢調査 | 90 | 雇用者数を少なめに申告する | 34 |
| 公団 | 19 | 国勢調査局 | 90 | | |
| 交通費 | 38 | 国内総生産 | 18 | ゴロ | 188 |
| 公定歩合 | 16 | 酷評する | 165 | コロコロ変わる | 104 |
| 公的資金 | 27 | 国民総生産 | 18 | ゴロを打つ | 188 |
| 高騰 | 54 | 国民的合意 | 132 | ゴロをはじく | 189 |
| 高騰する | 54 | 国民投票 | 84 | 懇請 | 132 |
| 行動する | 17 | 国民年金 | 37 | コントロールが悪い[良い] | 180 |
| | | 国務長官 | 100 | | |

# 日本語索引

| | | | | | |
|---|---|---|---|---|---|
| コントロールの抜群にい | | 最先端技術 | 150 | 三権分立 | 126 |
| いピッチャー | 179 | 採択 | 131 | 三振 | 177 |
| 困難 | 31 | 採択する | 131 | 三振する | 178 |
| コンピュータウイルス | | 在宅介護 | 160 | 三振に打ちとる | 177 |
| | 153 | 最多勝投手 | 176 | 三大証券 | 59 |
| コンピュータ2000年問題 | | 最低税率 | 71 | 三打席目に | 185 |
| | 153 | 裁定取引 | 59 | 暫定軍事政権 | 98 |
| コンピュータの欠陥 | 153 | サイドスロー（投手）174 | | 暫定政権 | 98 |
| コンピュータを無力にす | | 歳入 | 133 | 暫定予算 | 134 |
| る | 154 | 采配を振る | 169 | 暫定予算 | 98 |
| コンベヤー | 152 | 財閥 | 51 | 惨敗 | 93 |
| 根本的原因 | 16 | 債務 | 26 | 散発6安打に抑える | 182 |
| 混乱 | 134 | 債務者 | 26 | 三塁 | 196 |
| 混乱する | 134 | 債務超過 | 32 | 三塁 | 185 |
| **さ** | | 債務不履行 | 27 | 三塁ゴロ | 188 |
| サードコーチャー | 194 | 債務返済能力 | 26 | 残塁させる | 186 |
| サードフライ | 187 | 最優遇貸出金利 | 29 | 三塁手を動けなくする | |
| 再開 | 128 | 最優先する | 120 | | 188 |
| 財界 | 51 | 最優先の課題 | 131 | 三塁線 | 191 |
| 最下位 | 170 | 最有力候補 | 87 | 三塁打 | 190 |
| 再開する | 128 | サインに首を振る | 182 | 三連勝 | 169 |
| サイクルヒット | 190 | さがり | 76 | **し** | |
| サイクルヒットを打つ | | 先細りになる | 27 | 地上げ屋 | 25 |
| | 190 | 先物取引 | 68 | 試合 | 132 |
| 債権 | 26 | 削除 | 152 | シーズンオフ | 168 |
| 債券 | 67 | 削除する | 152 | G7 | 48 |
| 再建計画 | 32 | 昨年に比べて | 46 | シートノック | 199 |
| 再建策 | 32 | 些細なことを大袈裟にす | | シーリング | 133 |
| 債権者 | 26 | る | 108 | 仕入れ原価 | 28 |
| 最高税率 | 71 | 些細なもめごと | 108 | 時価 | 61 |
| 最高の | 109 | 支える | 160 | 自画自賛する | 88 |
| 最高の人，物 | 109 | サッカーくじ | 163 | 時価総額 | 61 |
| 在庫を減らす | 39 | 左派 | 103 | 仕方ない | 119 |
| 最終利益 | 28 | 左翼 | 103 | 次官 | 102 |
| 歳出 | 133 | サヨナラホームラン | 192 | 市議会 | 128 |
| 最新の数字 | 62 | 三冠王 | 183 | 死球 | 181 |
| 最新のニュース | 115 | 参議院 | 126 | 四球 | 180 |
| 財政赤字 | 133 | 参議院議員 | 126 | 四球を与える | 180 |
| 財政黒字 | 133 | 三球三振 | 178 | 四球を選ぶ | 180 |
| 財政出動 | 16 | 産業の空洞化 | 48 | 四球を出す | 180 |

207

| | | | | | |
|---|---|---|---|---|---|
| 仕切る | 78 | 下手投げ投手 | 174 | 社会主義 | 99 |
| 資金集め | 89 | 自治（権） | 145 | 社会主義者 | 99 |
| 資金調達者 | 89 | 市長 | 84 | 社会通念 | 143 |
| 資金の流用 | 142 | 失業の可能性 | 35 | 社会的信用を失う | 30 |
| 資金不足の | 90 | 実権のない役職［人］ | 102 | 社会的信用を回復する | 30 |
| 資金を集める | 89 | 実施する | 136 | 社会の中核 | 145 |
| 施行する | 136 | 実質で | 64 | 社会民主党 | 105 |
| 自己資本 | 27 | 実質的利益 | 63 | しゃがむ | 78 |
| 自己資本比率 | 27 | 実物の模型 | 150 | 弱者 | 160 |
| 自分を売り込む | 88 | 実力者 | 108 | 市役所 | 128 |
| 自殺点 | 163 | 支店長 | 24 | 弱小政党 | 105 |
| 支持 | 90 | 指導者 | 104 | 弱体政権 | 98 |
| 支持者 | 90 | 指導力を発揮する | 112 | 社債 | 67 |
| 支持する | 90 | 死に体の | 98 | 借金 | 26 |
| 事実上の | 105 | 賜杯 | 81 | ジャンク・ボンド | 67 |
| 自主規制 | 47 | 支配者 | 97 | ジャンピングキャッチ | |
| 自由規制する | 47 | 支配する | 169 | | 196 |
| 支出 | 133 | 私腹を肥やす | 142 | 首位 | 171 |
| 自主独立主義者 | 103 | 自分のアイデアを押し売 | | 首位から引きずり下ろす | |
| 市場開放 | 48 | りする | 121 | | 171 |
| 市場価格を操作する | 51 | 司法 | 126 | 首位打者 | 183 |
| 市場経済 | 44 | 司法長官 | 100 | 首位チーム | 171 |
| 史上最悪の失業率 | 35 | 司法府 | 126 | 首位に返り咲く | 171 |
| 至上の | 109 | 資本家 | 98 | 首位になる | 171 |
| 市場の隙間 | 154 | 資本金 | 67 | 首位の | 171 |
| 市場は飽和状態だ | 15 | 資本主義 | 98 | 首位を守る | 171 |
| 市条令 | 135 | 資本主義者 | 98 | 収益が伸び悩む | 16 |
| 市場をこじ開ける | 48 | 資本提携 | 39 | 自由化 | 48 |
| 支持率 | 102 | 市民オンブズマン | 143 | 自由化する | 48 |
| 支持を取りつける | 90 | 自民党総裁 | 105 | 衆議院 | 126 |
| 自信満々 | 183 | 事務次官 | 102 | 衆議院議員 | 126 |
| 地滑り的勝利 | 93 | 指名 | 88 | 集計 | 92 |
| 自責点 | 182 | 指名候補 | 88 | 衆参両院 | 126 |
| 事前運動 | 88 | 指名する | 88 | 修辞 | 123 |
| 慈善活動 | 41 | 指名打者 | 184 | 収支が合う | 28 |
| 持続可能な成長 | 18 | 占めている | 51 | 重視する | 120 |
| 次第に減少していく | 112 | 地面すれすれでの捕球 | | 自由主義 | 103 |
| 下支えする | 18 | | 197 | 自由主義者 | 103 |
| 下手 | 78 | ジャージを脱ぎ捨てる | | 自由主義の | 103 |
| 下手投げ | 79 | | 163 | 修正 | 132 |

# 日本語索引

| | | | | | |
|---|---|---|---|---|---|
| 修正する | 132,134 | 出塁率 | 193 | 召集する | 128 |
| 修正を強く求める | 132 | 主導権 | 112 | 照準を合わせる | 89 |
| 集積回路 | 152 | 主導権争い | 112 | 上場株 | 60 |
| 重大性を帯びる | 119 | 主導権争いをする | 112 | 上場企業 | 60 |
| 重大な局面 | 118 | 主導権を失う | 112 | 上昇傾向にある | 63 |
| 住宅投資 | 19 | 主導権を握る | 112 | 正真正銘の（誠実な）党 | |
| シュート | 177 | 首都機能移転 | 145 | 員 | 105 |
| 充当する | 27 | 守備 | 196 | 情勢が厳しくなった | 118 |
| 収入 | 133 | 守備練習 | 199 | 女性人権擁護団体 | 158 |
| 就任 | 99 | 主要銘柄 | 60 | 小選挙区（制） | 86 |
| 就任させる | 99 | 需要 | 18 | 小選挙区比例代表並立制 | |
| 就任式 | 99 | 主流派 | 107 | | 86 |
| 醜聞 | 142 | 春季キャンプ | 168 | 省庁 | 144 |
| 醜聞をあさる | 142 | 準決勝（戦） | 163 | 衝突する（こと） | 64 |
| 周辺機器 | 152 | 俊足の選手 | 193 | ショートバウンド | 197 |
| 自由貿易 | 44 | 春闘 | 35 | 性に合わない | 41 |
| 自由貿易体制への道を開 | | 純益 | 28 | 承認 | 130 |
| く | 44 | 小委員会 | 127 | 承認する | 130 |
| 自由放任政策 | 44 | 上位打線 | 183 | 消費者が元気を取り戻し | |
| 自由民主党 | 105 | 上院 | 129 | つつある | 19 |
| 住民税 | 70 | 上院議員 | 129 | 消費者物価 | 18 |
| 収賄する | 140 | 上映 | 164 | 消費税 | 70 |
| 自由を妨げるもの | 161 | 上映する | 164 | 勝負強い打者 | 184 |
| 受益者 | 140 | 償還 | 67 | 商法 | 58 |
| 熟達さ | 153 | 商慣行 | 49 | 情報開示 | 26 |
| 熟達した | 153 | 商業地 | 70 | 商法改正 | 58 |
| 熟達者 | 153 | 条件 | 40 | 情報公開 | 26 |
| 主計局 | 132 | 証券化 | 68 | 情報の暗号化 | 154 |
| 主権 | 98 | 証券会社 | 59 | 情報を開示する | 26 |
| 首相 | 101 | 証券化する | 68 | 情報を公開する | 26 |
| 受賞者 | 165 | 証券取引法 | 58 | 消滅した | 31 |
| 首相代理 | 101 | 証券取引委員会 | 58 | 勝利打点 | 192 |
| 首相の座に就く | 101 | 小康（状態） | 66 | 勝利投手 | 175 |
| 首長国 | 97 | 条項 | 136 | 省略 | 137 |
| 出現 | 143 | 詳細は明らかにされなか | | 省略する | 137 |
| 出産奨励策 | 158 | った | 39 | 条令 | 135 |
| 出生率 | 158 | 小差で | 93 | 条令を発する | 135 |
| 出生率の低下 | 158 | 少子化 | 158 | 除外する | 163 |
| 出馬する | 87 | 商社 | 46 | 職業安定所 | 160 |
| 出塁する | 193 | 召集 | 128 | 職業倫理 | 30 |

209

| | | | | | |
|---|---|---|---|---|---|
| 食費 | 38 | 新国民生活指標 | 14 | スライダー | 177 |
| 職務権限 | 141 | 信条 | 104 | スリーラン | 191 |
| 受勲者 | 165 | 新人候補 | 87 | **せ** | |
| 殊勲賞 | 81 | 新設企業 | 155 | 請願 | 140 |
| 叙勲制度 | 165 | 信託銀行 | 23 | 税金回避地 | 73 |
| 助成金 | 140 | 死んだふりをする | 113 | 税金が高い | 71 |
| 助成金を支給する | 140 | 侵入 | 153 | 税金が安い | 71 |
| 所得税 | 70 | 侵入する | 153 | 政権党 | 104 |
| 庶民 | 102 | 信任投票 | 92 | 政権に返り咲く | 100 |
| (署名などの) サイン | 182 | 信用金庫 | 24 | 政権に就く | 100 |
| 所有者 | 25 | 信用組合 | 24 | 政権を握っている | 100 |
| 知らせる | 136 | 信用できない | 107 | 制限を設ける | 47 |
| 尻込みする | 140 | 信用できる | 107 | 税控除 | 71 |
| 時流 | 114 | 信用取引 | 59 | 政策転換 | 56 |
| 時流に逆らって | 114 | 信用ならない | 117 | 政策立案者 | 127 |
| 時流に乗って | 114 | 信用を傷つける | 143 | 清算 | 32 |
| シルバー人材センター | | **す** | | 清算する | 32 |
| | 160 | 崇高な理念 | 104 | 正式な手続き | 132 |
| 試練 | 31 | 数字上の平均 | 36 | 政治的影響力 | 109 |
| 人員過剰問題 | 34 | 趨勢 | 114 | 政治的影響力を高める | |
| 人員削減 | 34 | スーパー 301 条 | 49 | | 109 |
| 侵害する | 151 | スーパースターを確保する | | 政治的手腕 | 112 |
| 審議 | 129 | | 164 | 政治的な取引をする | 113 |
| 審議会 | 127 | 隙間市場 | 154 | 政治的な紛糾を切り抜ける | |
| 新技術に遅れずについて | | スクイズ (する) | 186 | | 135 |
| いく | 150 | 救い主 | 143 | 政治不信 | 107 |
| 審議する | 129 | すぐピッチャーを替える | | 税収 | 71 |
| 新規補充をしない | 34 | 監督 [コーチ] | 175 | 税制改革 | 72 |
| シングルキャッチ | 196 | スクリューボール | 177 | 税制調査会 | 72 |
| シングルヒット | 189 | ストックオプション | 59 | 税制優遇措置 | 72 |
| 神経ガス | 162 | ストップ高 | 63 | 政調会長 | 106 |
| 人権蹂躙 | 131 | ストップ安 | 63 | 成長しうるビジネス | 154 |
| 人件費 | 38 | ストライキ | 177 | 静電気 | 152 |
| 新興市場 | 48 | ストレートの四球 | 181 | 政党 | 104 |
| 人工芝 | 168 | 頭脳流出 | 150 | 青年会議所 | 51 |
| 進行中の | 130 | スピンオフ | 40 | 政府高官 | 102 |
| 人口統計 | 91 | すべり止め | 195 | 税負担 | 70 |
| 人口統計の | 91 | 住みにくい社会 | 161 | 政府の誤った経済政策 | 16 |
| 人口流出 | 86 | (相撲) 部屋 | 76 | 成文法 | 135 |
| 人口流入 | 86 | 相撲をとる | 76 | 生保 | 24 |

| | | | | | |
|---|---|---|---|---|---|
| 生命保険会社 | 24 | 選挙区 | 86 | 送金（手段） | 27 |
| 誓約 | 89 | 選挙結果 | 92 | 送金する | 27 |
| 整理回収銀行 | 32 | 選挙権 | 84 | 相互依存 | 44 |
| 税理士 | 70 | 選挙参謀 | 88 | 相互依存の | 44 |
| 税率 | 71 | 選挙事務所 | 89 | 相互作用 | 153 |
| （整理）統合する | 144 | 選挙制度 | 84 | 相互に作用する | 153 |
| 精力的な | 108 | 選挙人名簿 | 90 | 総裁選 | 105 |
| セーブ（ポイント）をあげる | 175 | 選挙民 | 90 | 相殺する | 26 |
| 世界の恋人 | 164 | 先見の明のある人 | 156 | 増資 | 67 |
| 世界貿易機構 | 49 | 潜在能力 | 155 | 増資する | 67 |
| 世界を股にかける企業 | 20 | 前日比 | 61 | 贈収賄（事件） | 140 |
| 関取 | 77 | 前日比100円高［安］ | 61 | 相乗効果 | 17 |
| 責任逃れ | 143 | （選手などの）サイン | 182 | 増税 | 72 |
| 関脇 | 78 | 漸進主義 | 103 | 総選挙 | 84 |
| セクハラ | 36 | 前進守備の | 196 | 相続税 | 70 |
| 世間知らず | 87 | 宣誓 | 99 | 相対主義 | 97 |
| 施行 | 136 | 宣誓する | 99 | 増長している | 154 |
| 是正措置 | 30 | 専制政治 | 97 | 挿入 | 152 |
| 積極的な | 155 | センター前 | 191 | 挿入する | 152 |
| 折衝する | 133 | 全体主義 | 99 | 相場 | 61 |
| 摂食障害 | 162 | 全体主義者 | 99 | 造反者 | 117 |
| 接戦の | 92 | 前代未聞の | 118 | 造反する | 117 |
| 絶対過半数 | 93 | 先端技術 | 150 | 双方向の | 153 |
| 絶対君主 | 96 | 遷都 | 145 | 総務会長 | 106 |
| 絶対主義 | 97 | 先頭 | 104 | 贈与税 | 70 |
| 設備過剰 | 19 | 先頭打者 | 183 | 走塁 | 193 |
| 設備投資 | 19 | 前任者をたたえる | 99 | 贈賄（事件） | 140 |
| 説明責任 | 144 | 前年同月比 | 46 | 組閣する | 101 |
| ゼネコン | 25 | 前年同月比で | 46 | 族議員 | 140 |
| せり勝つ | 170 | 先発投手 | 174 | 促進 | 23 |
| ゼロ成長 | 17 | 先発投手に襲いかかる | 190 | 促進する | 23 |
| 善意に満ちた | 123 | 前編 | 164 | 速度を早める | 22 |
| 前回の優勝者 | 163 | 専門委員会 | 127 | 束縛 | 161 |
| 選球眼 | 184 | **そ** | | 底を打つ | 65 |
| 選球眼のいい打者 | 184 | 増益 | 28 | 側近 | 100 |
| 選挙 | 84 | 総会屋 | 58 | 側近の人々 | 100 |
| 選挙違反 | 86 | 総会屋対策を講ずる | 58 | 即効 | 17 |
| 選挙運動 | 88 | 総会屋と手を切る | 58 | 速球 | 176 |
| 選挙管理委員会 | 85 | 送球でアウトにする | 194 | 速球投手 | 177 |
| | | | | 速球を打ち返す | 186 |

| | | | | | |
|---|---|---|---|---|---|
| 外掛け | 79 | 台無しにする | 30 | 脱税を阻止する | 73 |
| その逆 | 40 | 台無しにする | 131 | 脱線させる | 131 |
| その調子だ | 183 | 大評判をとる | 116 | タッチアウトにする | 194 |
| その場しのぎの数字を並べる | 34 | ダイビングキャッチ | 196 | タッチアップする | 194 |
| | | 大本命 | 87 | タッチを避ける | 194 |
| それとなくほのめかす | 123 | タイムリーヒット | 189 | 脱落させる | 163 |
| | | 大躍進（で） | 155 | 打点 | 192 |
| そろばん | 151 | 対立候補 | 88 | たなぼた | 29 |
| 損益計算書 | 29 | 対立候補より多く金を使う | 90 | 狸寝入りをする | 113 |
| 損益分岐点 | 28 | | | だぶだぶのズボン | 160 |
| 損害保険会社 | 24 | 大量消費 | 19 | ＷＴＯ | 49 |
| 村議会 | 128 | 大量生産 | 19 | ダブル[トリプル]プレー | 196 |
| 尊敬すべき | 109 | 対若乃花戦 | 78 | | |
| 存在理由 | 112 | ダウ平均 | 62 | ダブルプレーをする | 196 |
| 損失 | 65 | 絶えず（不規則に）変化する | 54 | 球が甘い | 179 |
| 損失補てん | 65 | | | だます | 117 |
| 損保 | 24 | 絶え間ない不安 | 66 | だらしな系ファッション | 160 |
| **た** | | 高い出塁率 | 193 | | |
| 退位 | 96 | 高い投票率 | 91 | 打率 | 183 |
| 退位する | 96 | 高値 | 61 | たわごと | 122 |
| 大改革 | 39 | タカ派 | 104 | 弾劾 | 101 |
| 大河小説 | 165 | タカ派の | 104 | 弾劾する | 101 |
| 戴冠式 | 96 | 高目のボールを狙う | 186 | 段階的に整理する | 26 |
| 大差で | 93 | 抱き込む | 113 | 嘆願する | 140 |
| 大衆 | 102 | たきつける | 121 | 弾丸ライナー | 187 |
| 大臣 | 101 | 卓越した | 109 | 探究 | 150 |
| 大臣の職 | 102 | 託児所不足 | 158 | 団結 | 35 |
| 大臣を任命する | 101 | 宅地 | 70 | 談合 | 50 |
| 大接戦 | 92 | 打撃 | 196 | 断固たる | 130 |
| 大接戦を演じる | 92 | 打撃練習 | 199 | 断固たる決意 | 112 |
| 大胆な | 34 | 多国籍企業 | 20 | 単純化する | 144 |
| 大店法 | 50 | 出し抜く | 117 | 単純平均 | 36 |
| 大統領 | 99 | 打順 | 183 | 男女雇用機会均等法 | 36 |
| 大統領執務室 | 100 | 打席 | 185 | 単身赴任 | 158 |
| 大統領選 | 84 | 打席に入る | 185 | 単身赴任者 | 158 |
| 大統領選に立候補する | 87 | 立ち合い | 78 | 団体交渉 | 35 |
| 大統領特権 | 101 | 立ち上がる | 78 | 堪能さ | 153 |
| 大統領報道官 | 100 | 立場が逆転した | 118 | ダンピング | 48 |
| 大統領補佐官 | 100 | 脱税 | 72 | ダンピング防止税 | 48 |
| 大統領令 | 136 | 脱税する | 73 | 担保 | 25 |

# 日本語索引

## ち

| | |
|---|---|
| 地位 | 77 |
| チームを率いる | 169 |
| 遅延の | 26 |
| 地価 | 25 |
| 誓う | 89 |
| 地価税 | 70 |
| 地下鉄サリン事件 | 162 |
| 地価の下落 | 25 |
| 力いっぱい振る | 186 |
| 蓄財 | 142 |
| 蓄財する | 142 |
| 知事 | 84 |
| 知事選 | 84 |
| 知的所有権 | 151 |
| 血は水よりも濃い | 97 |
| 地方議会 | 127 |
| 地方銀行 | 23 |
| 地方自治 | 145 |
| 地方自治体 | 145 |
| 地方税 | 70 |
| 地方分権 | 145 |
| 地方分権を行う | 145 |
| 地方遊説 | 89 |
| 地方を遊説する | 88 |
| 地歩を得る | 114 |
| チャンスはまだいくらでもある | 119 |
| 注意を喚起する | 141 |
| 仲介会社 | 59 |
| 中核 | 145 |
| 中間選挙 | 85 |
| 中継プレー | 197 |
| 中堅の | 59 |
| 中産階級 | 72 |
| 中傷 | 121 |
| 中所得者層 | 72 |
| 中枢 | 107 |
| 中枢の | 107 |
| 中断 | 169 |
| 中断した | 169 |
| 中道左派（の） | 103 |
| 中道主義 | 103 |
| 中道政権 | 103 |
| 中道政党 | 105 |
| 中道の | 103 |
| 注入 | 27 |
| 注入する | 27 |
| 注文（する） | 60 |
| 中立 | 103 |
| 中立主義 | 103 |
| 中立にとどまる | 103 |
| 中立の | 103 |
| 懲戒（する） | 35 |
| 懲戒処分 | 35 |
| 懲戒免職 | 35 |
| 超過する | 32 |
| 長官 | 100,101 |
| 町議会 | 128 |
| 長期信用銀行 | 23 |
| 長距離打者 | 184 |
| 帳消しにする | 26 |
| 超豪華な | 165 |
| 調子が出てきた | 183 |
| 調子が悪い [いい] | 182 |
| 徴税 | 71 |
| 長打 | 190 |
| 長打する | 190 |
| 長打率 | 190 |
| 超党派（の） | 105 |
| 帳簿外の | 30 |
| 帳簿をごまかす | 29 |
| 帳簿を照合する | 30 |
| 跳躍台 | 114 |
| 潮流 | 114 |
| 長老 | 108 |
| 直接税 | 70 |
| 直流 | 152 |
| 直列 | 152 |
| 著作権 | 151 |
| 著作権侵害 | 151 |
| 著作権侵害者 | 151 |
| 著作権法 | 151 |
| 著作権を侵害する | 151 |
| 直球 | 176 |
| 賃上げ要求 | 36 |
| 沈思黙考する | 120 |

## つ

| | |
|---|---|
| （通貨を）切り上げる | 56 |
| （通貨を）切り下げる | 56 |
| 通算本塁打 | 192 |
| 通常国会 | 127 |
| ツー・スリー | 179 |
| 突き出す | 79 |
| 月並みな映画 | 164 |
| 都合のよい | 123 |
| 伝える | 152 |
| 土 | 77 |
| つなぎ融資 | 32 |
| 綱引 | 112 |
| つまらない喧嘩をする | 121 |
| 積立金 | 37 |
| 強いゴロ | 188 |
| 強気な | 65 |
| 強気な人 | 65 |
| 釣り合い | 116 |
| 釣り合わせる | 116 |
| つり出す | 79 |

## て

| | |
|---|---|
| 提携 | 39 |
| 提携する | 39 |
| 低姿勢を保つ | 115 |
| 提出 | 129 |
| 低所得者層 | 72 |
| 定数 | 150 |
| 停滞した | 15 |
| 抵当 | 25 |
| 低迷する自動車販売 | 15 |
| データ処理 | 152 |

213

| | | | | | |
|---|---|---|---|---|---|
| 手形 | 32 | 党推薦候補 | 87 | トスバッティング | 199 |
| 出来高 | 61 | 当選確実な人 | 87 | 特許(権) | 151 |
| 出口調査 | 91 | 当選する | 93 | 特許権侵害 | 151 |
| テクノロジーが法律を追い越している | 151 | 当選を無効にする | 93 | 突破する | 78 |
| でたらめ | 122 | 党大会 | 85 | トップバッター | 183 |
| 徹底して支持する | 90 | 同調して | 114 | とてつもなく大きな影響 | 150 |
| デッドボール | 181 | 同調しないで | 114 | 都道府県条令 | 135 |
| デリバティブ | 67 | 盗聴法案 | 129 | 滞らせる | 134 |
| 電子マネー | 154 | 同点 | 170 | とにかく | 38 |
| 伝導 | 152 | 頭取 | 23 | 土俵 | 76 |
| 店頭株 | 60 | (党内)左派 | 107 | 土俵入り | 76 |
| 天然資源 | 47 | 党内の激しい駆引 | 107 | 土俵を割る | 79 |
| 電流 | 152 | 導入 | 119 | とぼける | 113 |

**と**

| | | | | | |
|---|---|---|---|---|---|
| 統一地方選 | 84 | 党派主義 | 104 | ドラッグバント | 186 |
| 同一労働同一賃金 | 36 | 登板する | 175 | 取組 | 78 |
| 党員集会 | 85 | 投票 | 91 | 取り消し | 137 |
| 投機 | 59 | 投票する | 91 | 取り消す | 136 |
| 動議 | 129 | 投票にかける | 130 | 取り除く | 117 |
| 投機筋 | 59 | 投票用紙 | 91 | 取引されている | 55 |
| 投機する | 59 | 投票率 | 91 | 取引高 | 61 |
| 投機的な | 59 | ドーピング | 163 | 取引をする | 113 |
| 動議は可決されました | 130 | 同部屋の力士 | 76 | 取りまき | 100 |
| 東京証券取引所 | 61 | 同胞 | 106 | ドルが円に対して | 55 |
| 東京都知事 | 84 | 遠回しの言及 | 123 | ドル建て債 | 67 |
| 凍結(する) | 137 | 透明性 | 26 | ドル建ての | 67 |
| 統合 | 144 | 到来 | 143 | トレーニング | 198 |
| 党公認候補 | 87 | 党利党略 | 104 | トンネル会社 | 30 |
| 洞察力 | 156 | 盗塁(する) | 193 | トンネルする | 198 |
| 洞察力のある | 156 | 都議会 | 128 | | |

**な**

| | | | | | |
|---|---|---|---|---|---|
| 倒産 | 31 | 独裁者 | 97 | 内閣 | 101 |
| 倒産する | 31 | 独裁制 | 97 | 内閣改造 | 101 |
| 導師 | 109 | 独裁政権 | 97 | 内閣官房長官 | 101 |
| 投資信託(会社) | 68 | 独占禁止法 | 50 | 内角高目 | 178 |
| 投資への熱意 | 66 | 徳俵 | 76 | 内角低目 | 178 |
| 投手陣 | 174 | 特別国会 | 127 | 内角へ食い込む | 179 |
| 東証一部上場企業 | 60 | 特別審議会 | 127 | 内角へ投げる | 179 |
| 東証指数 | 62 | 独立検察官 | 101 | 内需 | 18 |
| | | 都市銀行 | 23 | 内需拡大 | 18 |
| | | 都市のスプロール現象 | 145 | 内情に通じている | 114 |

# 日本語索引

| | | | | | |
|---|---|---|---|---|---|
| ナイター | 169 | 日経平均 | 62 | 根回しをする | 112 |
| 内部情報 | 65 | 日経連 | 51 | 狙い打ちする打者 | 184 |
| 内部の人間 | 65 | 2点タイムリー | 189 | 年金基金 | 37 |
| 内野安打 | 189 | 二度あることは三度ある | 155 | (年金の)支払い | 37 |
| 内野ゴロを足でヒットにする | 189 | 二敗目を喫する | 80 | 年2回の | 29 |
| 内野手のあいだを抜けるヒット | 189 | 日本銀行 | 23 | **の** | |
| 内野席 | 168 | 日本経営者団体連盟 | 51 | ノーコンだ | 180 |
| 内野フライ | 187 | 日本商工会議所 | 51 | 納税者 | 70 |
| 流し打ち | 184 | 日本相撲協会 | 76 | 納税申告(書) | 70 |
| 流し打ちのヒット | 184 | 日本版401kプラン | 37 | ノート型パソコン | 151 |
| 流し打つ | 184 | 入札 | 50 | ノーヒットノーラン | 176 |
| 中継ぎ投手 | 175 | 入札者 | 50 | ノーベル賞受賞者 | 165 |
| 中継ぎ投手陣 | 175 | 入札する | 50 | ノック | 199 |
| 長びく不況 | 15 | 入札手続き | 50 | 乗っ取り | 40 |
| 中へ入る | 79 | ニュースの要約 | 115 | 乗っ取る | 40 |
| 流れ | 114 | ニューヨーク証券取引所 | 61 | 野村証券 | 59 |
| 流れを変えた | 170 | | | 乗るかそるかの賭け | 59 |
| 投げ倒す | 79 | 二塁打 | 190 | ノンバンク | 23 |
| 投げを打つ | 79 | 二塁へ進塁する | 193 | **は** | |
| 名指しで非難する | 122 | 任期 | 99 | 廃止 | 144 |
| ナスダック複合指数 | 62 | 人気に火がついた | 161 | 廃止する | 144 |
| ナックルボール | 177 | 人間工学 | 150 | 買収 | 40 |
| 成り行きを見守る | 115 | **ぬ** | | 買収する | 40,140 |
| 縄張り | 144 | 抜き打ち選挙 | 84 | 背信行為 | 117 |
| 縄張り争い | 144 | 抜け穴 | 73 | 敗戦投手 | 175 |
| 難局 | 118 | **ね** | | 配当 | 63 |
| 難題 | 119 | 値上がり | 54 | 背任 | 30 |
| 難問 | 120 | 値上がり株 | 61 | 売買委託手数料 | 59 |
| 難問を解決する | 120 | 値上がりする | 54,62 | 売買代金 | 61 |
| 何らかの形で | 38 | 寝返る | 117 | 売買手数料 | 59 |
| **に** | | ネクストバッターズサークル | 185 | 売買の材料 | 66 |
| 二極化 | 44 | | | 馬鹿げた | 123 |
| 二極化する | 44 | 値下がり | 54 | 波及効果 | 17 |
| 2000年問題 | 153 | 値下がり株 | 61 | 波及効果をもたらす | 17 |
| 日銀 | 23 | 値下がりする | 54,64 | 白紙に戻す | 132 |
| 日銀総裁 | 23 | 熱心な | 90 | 激しい抗議 | 135 |
| 日銀短観 | 14 | ネット裏の席 | 168 | はじく | 198 |
| 日米構造協議 | 49 | 熱弁をふるう演説者 | 89 | 初めから決まっている結論 | 135 |
| | | 粘り強い企業家 | 155 | 始値 | 61 |

| | | | | | |
|---|---|---|---|---|---|
| 場所 | 77 | 番付（表） | 77 | 肥大化した官僚組織 | 144 |
| パスボール | 181 | 判定のストライク | 177 | 左投手 | 174 |
| はたき込む | 79 | 反動 | 117 | 微調整 | 64 |
| 破綻 | 31 | 半導体 | 152 | ピッチャーゴロ | 188 |
| 破綻した日本債権信用銀行 | 30 | バント（する） | 186 | ヒットエンドラン | 186 |
| 破綻する | 30 | 反トラスト法 | 50 | 引っぱり専門の打者 | 185 |
| 破綻せずにいる | 31 | 販売が上昇した | 17 | 必要経費 | 38 |
| バックネット | 168 | 反ばくする | 121 | 一人当たり | 29 |
| バックホーム（する） | 197 | 反発する | 65 | ひとり占めする | 50 |
| 発行済株式 | 58 | 氾濫 | 150 | ひとりで暮らす老人 | 160 |
| 発行する | 67 | **ひ** | | 一人につき | 29 |
| 発効する | 136 | ピークに達する | 63 | 人をだますような | 117 |
| バッティング投手 | 175 | PK戦 | 163 | 非難する | 122 |
| 発展の可能性のある新設企業 | 155 | ビーンボール | 181 | 非難を招く | 143 |
| | | 非営利団体 | 51 | 否認 | 131 |
| バットの芯 | 186 | 非課税の | 71 | 否認する | 131 |
| バットを短めに持つ | 186 | 悲観材料 | 65 | 非武装中立 | 103 |
| 発布 | 135 | 非関税障壁 | 46 | 誹謗者 | 122 |
| 八方ふさがり | 118 | 悲観論が広がっている | 66 | 誹謗する | 122 |
| ハト派 | 104 | 引き金を引く | 64 | 秘密研究開発部門 | 150 |
| ハト派の | 104 | 引締策 | 16 | 秘密試写会 | 165 |
| 派閥 | 106 | 引き締める | 16 | 秘密の | 142 |
| 派閥争い | 107 | 引き倒す | 79 | 罷免 | 101 |
| 派閥間の対決 | 107 | 引き分け | 170 | 罷免する | 101 |
| 派閥主義 | 106 | 引く | 78 | 票差 | 93 |
| バブル経済 | 14 | 火消し | 175 | 票のごまかし | 92 |
| バブル経済の崩壊 | 14 | ピケ隊 | 36 | 評判を落とす | 143 |
| 早くとも | 17 | 否決 | 131 | 日和見を決め込む | 115 |
| 払い戻す | 67 | 否決する | 131 | ひらめいた | 156 |
| パラダイム | 119 | ひけらかす | 88 | 比例代表制 | 86 |
| バランスを保つ | 45 | ピケを張る | 36 | 広く行き渡った | 161 |
| 張り合う | 119 | 膝パッド | 195 | 広く行き渡る | 161 |
| はり手 | 78 | 肘鉄を食わせる | 116 | 品位 | 122 |
| ハワイ出身の | 77 | 非主流派 | 107 | 品位を落とすような | 122 |
| 反感を抱かせる | 122 | 非上場株 | 60 | 品性 | 122 |
| 犯罪行為 | 141 | 非常に高い目標 | 104 | **ふ** | |
| 反主流派 | 107 | 非常に有力な候補 | 87 | ファーストミット | 195 |
| 反対者 | 121 | 非政治的な | 103 | ファール | 177 |
| 番付の上［下］の力士 | 77 | 被選挙権 | 84 | ファールチップ | 177 |
| | | 砒素 | 162 | | |

# 日本語索引

| | | |
|---|---|---|
| ファイバーオプティクス | | 151 |
| ファウルグラウンド | | 168 |
| ファウルになりそうです | | 187 |
| ファウルに逃れる | | 186 |
| ファウルフライ | | 187 |
| ファンブルする | | 198 |
| 風俗産業 | | 162 |
| フェアグラウンド | | 168 |
| フォアボール | | 180 |
| フォークボール | | 177 |
| フォースアウトにする | | 194 |
| 付加価値 | | 47 |
| 不可抗力 | | 41 |
| 不況 | | 15 |
| 不協和音 | | 107 |
| 副幹事長 | | 105 |
| 福祉で最低限の生活をする | | 160 |
| 副首相 | | 101 |
| 副総裁 | | 105 |
| 副大統領 | | 99 |
| 副大統領候補 | | 88 |
| 副長官 | | 100 |
| 不屈の精神 | | 109 |
| 含み益 | | 28 |
| 含み損 | | 28 |
| 袋小路 | | 118 |
| 不景気 | | 15 |
| 布告する | | 136 |
| 負債 | | 26 |
| 不在者投票 | | 91 |
| ふさわしくない | | 49 |
| 婦人参政権 | | 84 |
| 不信任動議（案） | | 135 |
| 不信任動議案をうまくかわす | | 135 |
| 不信任投票 | | 92 |
| 不正行為 | | 141 |
| 不正支出 | | 141 |
| 不正融資 | | 24 |
| 防ぐ | | 162 |
| 不戦勝（する） | | 80 |
| 不戦敗 | | 80 |
| 不戦敗する | | 80 |
| 付属のマーケット | | 154 |
| 不遜な | | 122 |
| 舞台裏の | | 112 |
| 二桁勝利投手 | | 176 |
| 二桁のインフレ | | 20 |
| 負担する | | 26 |
| 普通株 | | 60 |
| 普通選挙権 | | 84 |
| 物価 | | 18 |
| 物議をかもす | | 116 |
| 物質的社会 | | 161 |
| 不動産 | | 25 |
| 不動産開発業者 | | 25 |
| 不動産業者 | | 25 |
| 腐敗 | | 142 |
| 腐敗した | | 142 |
| 腐敗して機能しなくなった | | 142 |
| 腐敗を一掃する | | 143 |
| 不抜の忍耐力 | | 109 |
| 不文法 | | 135 |
| 不平不満 | | 102 |
| 不法侵入（する） | | 154 |
| 不満な | | 102 |
| 不満を抱いた | | 102 |
| 武勇伝 | | 165 |
| 扶養控除 | | 71 |
| フライ | | 187 |
| プライバシーの保護 | | 154 |
| フライを打ち上げる | | 187 |
| ブラッシュボール | | 181 |
| フーリガン | | 163 |
| 不履行 | | 30 |
| 不利になる | | 180 |
| 不良債権 | | 25 |
| 不良債権の開示基準 | | 26 |
| 不良債権を管理する | | 26 |
| フルカウントから | | 180 |
| 無礼な | | 122 |
| 無礼な言動 | | 122 |
| プロテクター | | 195 |
| 不渡手形 | | 32 |
| 文化遺産 | | 166 |
| 文化勲章 | | 165 |
| 紛糾 | | 134 |
| 紛糾させる | | 134 |
| 分社 | | 40 |
| 分社化する | | 40 |
| 粉飾（決算） | | 29 |
| 分離 | | 144 |
| 分離課税 | | 71 |
| 分離する | | 144 |
| 分裂 | | 108 |
| 分裂する | | 108 |

## へ

| | |
|---|---|
| 閉会 | 128 |
| 閉会する | 128 |
| 並行輸入 | 44 |
| 米国債 | 67 |
| 平凡なフライ | 187 |
| 並列 | 152 |
| ベースに釘づけにする | 182 |
| ベースライン | 191 |
| ベースを踏み損なう | 194 |
| ヘッディング | 163 |
| ヘッドスライディング | 193 |
| 変化球 | 177 |
| 変革期 | 119 |
| 変動相場制 | 54 |
| 便法 | 123 |

## ほ

| 法案 | 129 |
| 法案を成立させる | 130 |
| 法案を棚上げする | 131 |
| 法案を提出する | 129 |
| 貿易赤字 | 45 |
| 貿易外取引 | 44 |
| 貿易黒字 | 45 |
| 貿易収支 | 45 |
| 貿易障壁 | 46 |
| 貿易不均衡 | 45 |
| 貿易摩擦 | 46 |
| 崩壊 | 118 |
| 妨害する | 44,162 |
| 傍観者 | 115 |
| 傍観する | 115 |
| 放棄試合 | 169 |
| 防御率 | 182 |
| 方向転換させる | 118 |
| 法人格 | 70 |
| 法人税 | 70 |
| 暴政 | 97 |
| 法的根拠 | 28 |
| 法的根拠を付する | 28 |
| 暴投 | 181 |
| 報道の自由 | 97 |
| 冒とく | 122 |
| 冒とくする | 122 |
| 法に従って | 58 |
| 報復関税 | 46 |
| 泡沫候補 | 87 |
| 暴落（する） | 64 |
| 法律的に無効な | 136 |
| 暴力をふるわれた妻 | 159 |
| ボーク（をする） | 182 |
| ホームインする | 195 |
| ホームページ | 153 |
| ホームラン | 191 |
| ホームランバッター | 184 |
| ホームランボール | 179 |

| ホームランを打つ | 191 |
| ボールから目を離す | 198 |
| ボールの縫い目 | 196 |
| ボールに当てる | 186 |
| ボールを落とす | 198 |
| ボールをたたきつける | 186 |
| ボーンヘッド | 198 |
| 捕球する | 196 |
| 補欠選挙 | 85 |
| ポケベル | 161 |
| 保護主義 | 44 |
| 保護貿易 | 44 |
| 保護貿易主義者 | 44 |
| 保守主義 | 103 |
| 保守的な | 103 |
| 保証人 | 25 |
| 補助金 | 140 |
| 星を五分に戻す | 80 |
| ポストをめぐるえこひいき | 102 |
| 母体保護法 | 158 |
| 補正予算 | 134 |
| 没収試合 | 169 |
| ポップフライ | 187 |
| ポップフライを打ち上げる | 187 |
| ポテンヒット | 189 |
| ポテンヒットを打つ | 189 |
| ほのめかし | 123 |
| 保母 | 158 |
| ボランティア活動 | 41 |
| ボランティア活動をする | 41 |
| 保留 | 131 |
| 保留にする | 131 |
| ボロ儲けする | 63 |
| 本会議 | 127 |
| 本質的な | 120 |
| 本調子を出す | 183 |

| 本末転倒だ | 117 |
| 本命 | 87 |
| 本塁打 | 191 |

## ま

| マーケットに活気がない | 66 |
| マイカー普及率 | 19 |
| マイナス成長 | 17 |
| マイナスに働く | 17 |
| 前頭一枚目 | 78 |
| 前触れになる | 118 |
| 前へ出る | 78 |
| 負かす | 93 |
| 巻き込む | 117 |
| まげ | 76 |
| まだ勝ち星のない | 80 |
| 間違っている | 121 |
| 間近に迫っている | 118 |
| まっ逆さまの | 23 |
| 抹殺する | 117 |
| まっしぐらの | 23 |
| まったくの | 122 |
| 的外れ | 112 |
| 的はずれの発言 | 123 |
| 麻痺させる | 135 |
| 麻痺状態 | 118 |
| マレーシア連邦 | 97 |
| まわし | 76 |
| まわしを取る | 78 |
| 真ん中 | 178 |
| マンネリだ | 110 |
| 満塁 | 194 |
| 満塁にする | 194 |
| 満塁ホームラン | 192 |

## み

| 見送りの三振をする | 178 |
| 未解決の | 131 |
| 未確認情報 | 65 |
| 右投手 | 174 |
| 右にかわる | 78 |

218

| | | | | | |
|---|---|---|---|---|---|
| 未婚の母 | 158 | 無党派(の) | 85,105 | もみ消し(工作) | 65 |
| 未償還債 | 67 | 無得点 | 195 | もみ消す | 65 |
| 水増し | 133 | 無認可保育園 | 158 | 問題外だ | 112 |
| 水増しする | 133 | 無任所大臣 | 102 | 問題に取り組む | 120 |
| 水増し請求 | 133 | 胸の高さのボール | 181 | 問題の核心 | 120 |
| 水増し要求 | 133 | 無分別 | 123 | **や** | |
| 未然に防ぐ | 15 | 村役場 | 128 | 八百長試合 | 169 |
| みそぎ | 143 | 群れ | 106 | (野)球場 | 168 |
| 見直される | 37 | **め** | | 約束手形 | 32 |
| 見直し | 134 | 目新しいもの | 150 | 役立たず | 102 |
| 見直す | 134 | 銘柄 | 60 | 役割を引き受ける | 50 |
| 見習う | 109 | 迷宮 | 118 | 安値 | 61 |
| ミニ政党 | 105 | 名人 | 166 | 野党 | 104 |
| 見逃しの三振をする | 178 | 明敏な | 156 | 破る | 40,169 |
| 未払い残高 | 28 | 名目で | 64 | ヤンキーズに勝つ | 169 |
| 耳ざわりな | 121 | 目立たないでいる | 115 | **ゆ** | |
| 民営化 | 20 | メディアを回避する | 165 | URL | 153 |
| 民営化する | 20 | メディケア | 37 | 優位の側につく | 114 |
| 民間企業 | 20 | メディケイド | 37 | 優位を取り戻す | 114 |
| 民間投資 | 19 | 免職 | 34 | 有価証券 | 60 |
| 民主主義 | 98 | 免職にする | 34 | 遊休地 | 25 |
| 民主主義の | 98 | 免税の | 71 | 有権者 | 90 |
| 民主党 | 85 | 免責 | 143 | 有効な | 92 |
| 民主党員 | 85 | **も** | | 融資 | 24 |
| 民主党 | 105 | もうけもの | 29 | 融資基準 | 24 |
| 民族主義 | 99 | もしうまくいかなかった | | 融資限度枠 | 24 |
| 民族主義者 | 99 | ら | 155 | 融資する | 24 |
| **む** | | もしうまくいったら | 155 | 優勝争いが激しくなる | |
| 無効 | 93 | もち合った株 | 60 | | 171 |
| 無効とする | 93 | 持ち家率 | 19 | 優勝争いをしている | 81 |
| 無効な | 92 | 持ち株会社 | 58 | 優勝決定戦 | 81 |
| 無効にする | 136 | 持ち株比率 | 60 | 優勝する | 81,170 |
| 無作為抽出 | 91 | 持ち主が変わる | 40 | 遊説する | 88 |
| 無作為に | 91 | 最も重要な問題 | 119 | 優勢だ | 92 |
| 無所属(の) | 85,105 | もつれ試合 | 170 | 優勢になる | 114 |
| むずかしいいやなゴロ | | 元に戻す | 135 | 優先株 | 60 |
| | 189 | 元に戻る | 54,135 | 勇退する | 110 |
| 無税地 | 73 | 物思いに沈んだ | 120 | 有望な市場 | 154 |
| 無敵の | 20 | 物事の核心をついた | 120 | ゆうゆうの二塁打 | 190 |
| 無党派層 | 85 | モフ担 | 24 | 優良株 | 60 |

| | | | | | |
|---|---|---|---|---|---|
| 有料の | 160 | 予備的な | 88 | 利権 | 141 |
| 有力な | 107 | 余分な | 34 | 履行 | 136 |
| 有力な候補 | 87 | 読み取り機 | 154 | 履行する | 136 |
| 有力な勢力 | 107 | 読み取り機に通す | 154 | 離婚の件数が横ばいになる | 159 |
| 輸出制限 | 47 | 寄り切る | 79 | | |
| 輸出と輸入はそれぞれ | 45 | 寄り倒す | 79 | 離職（率） | 35 |
| 輸出割当て | 47 | 世論調査 | 91 | リスクをひどく嫌う社会 | 66 |
| 豊かさ指標 | 14 | 世論調査員 | 91 | | |
| 輸入制限 | 47 | 弱いゴロ | 188 | リストラ | 34 |
| 輸入を妨げる | 44 | 弱気な | 65 | リストラの対象になる | 34 |
| 弓取り式 | 77 | 弱気な人 | 65 | 立憲君主制 | 96 |
| **よ** | | 弱含みで推移している | 66 | 立候補する | 87 |
| 要点の繰り返し | 120 | 弱まる | 112 | 立法 | 126 |
| 要点を繰り返す | 120 | 4番打者 | 183 | 立法者 | 127 |
| 預金はすべて保護されます | 32 | 401(k)プランを軽視する | 37 | 立法府 | 126 |
| | | | | リニアモーターカー | 150 |
| 預金保険機構 | 31 | **ら** | | 利にさとい | 63 |
| よく考える | 120 | ライトオーバー | 191 | 利尿剤 | 163 |
| 横綱 | 77 | ライト線 | 190 | 利払い | 134 |
| 横手投げ投手 | 174 | ライナー | 187 | リベート | 141 |
| 横ばいが続いている | 15 | ライナーを打つ | 187 | リベラルな | 103 |
| 予算（案） | 132 | ライン際を固める | 196 | 利回り | 63 |
| 予算委員会 | 127 | 楽勝する | 170 | 流行はスーッと消えていく | 161 |
| 予算教書 | 129 | 落選する | 93 | | |
| 予算原案 | 133 | ラケットを短めに持つ | 186 | 流動資産 | 27 |
| 予算削減 | 134 | | | 留保利益 | 28 |
| 予算修正 | 134 | 落球（する） | 198 | 流用する | 142 |
| 予算審議 | 133 | LAN | 153 | 量産する | 19 |
| 予算折衝 | 133 | 乱打戦 | 190 | リリーフ投手 | 174 |
| 予算配分 | 134 | ランナー | 193 | 臨時国会 | 127 |
| 予算要求 | 133 | ランナー一 | 185 | 臨時審議会 | 127 |
| 予算を監督する | 132 | ランナーなし | 185 | 臨時政権 | 98 |
| 予算を均衡させる | 133 | ランニングホームラン | 191 | **る** | |
| 予算を削減する | 134 | | | 累進課税 | 71 |
| 余剰人員 | 34 | **り** | | 累進課税制度 | 71 |
| 余剰労働者 | 34 | リードして | 193 | 累積赤字 | 133 |
| 予選 | 163 | リードを取らせない | 182 | **れ** | |
| 与党 | 104 | 利益供与 | 141 | 例外なき関税化 | 46 |
| よどんだ | 15 | 利益団体 | 140 | 冷遇される | 117 |
| 予備選挙 | 84 | 力士 | 76 | 冷遇する | 117 |

| | | | |
|---|---|---|---|
| 零細企業 | 51 | **わ** | |
| 冷静でいる | 119 | 賄賂 | 140 |
| レガース | 195 | わけなく | 169 |
| 歴史的建造物の修復 | 166 | 分け前に預かる | 63 |
| 劣後ローン | 29 | 笑いを誘う | 123 |
| レトリック | 123 | | |
| 錬金術 | 155 | | |
| 錬金術師 | 155 | | |
| 連結決算 | 29 | | |
| 連勝 | 169 | | |
| 練習 | 198 | | |
| 連帯 | 35 | | |
| 連帯責任 | 143 | | |
| 連邦 | 97 | | |
| 連邦準備銀行 | 61 | | |
| 連邦準備制度理事会 | 61 | | |
| 連邦政府 | 97 | | |
| 連立政権 | 102 | | |
| **ろ** | | | |
| 老化 | 159 | | |
| 労災 | 36 | | |
| 労使関係 | 35 | | |
| 労使紛争 | 35 | | |
| 老人パワー | 160 | | |
| 老人病 | 160 | | |
| 老人ホーム | 160 | | |
| 老人問題 | 160 | | |
| 労働基準法 | 36 | | |
| 労働組合 | 35 | | |
| 労働争議 | 35 | | |
| 労務管理 | 36 | | |
| 老齢年金 | 37 | | |
| 労を惜しまない | 109 | | |
| 六連勝 | 80 | | |
| ロスタイム | 163 | | |
| ロビー活動 | 140 | | |
| ロビー活動をする | 140 | | |
| ロビイスト | 140 | | |
| ロングヒット | 190 | | |
| 論争を避ける | 121 | | |

# 英語索引

## A

| | | |
|---|---|---|
| A bird in the hand is worth two in the bush. | 113 | |
| a man of vision | 156 | |
| a shot in the arm | 17 | |
| abacus | 151 | |
| abbreviate | 137 | |
| abbreviation | 137 | |
| abdicate | 96 | |
| abdication | 96 | |
| abolish | 144 | |
| abolition | 144 | |
| abrasive | 121 | |
| absentee voting | 91 | |
| absolute majority | 93 | |
| absolute monarch | 96 | |
| absolutism | 97 | |
| absorb | 40 | |
| absorption | 40 | |
| abstain (from voting) | 91 | |
| abstention | 91 | |
| abuses of his power | 142 | |
| accelerate | 23 | |
| acceleration | 23 | |
| accept a bribe | 141 | |
| accomplished fact | 135 | |
| account for | 51 | |
| accountability | 144 | |
| accumulated deficit | 133 | |
| ace (pitcher) | 174 | |
| acquire | 60 | |
| acquisition | 60 | |
| acting prime minister | 101 | |
| acumen | 156 | |
| ad hoc council | 127 | |
| adamant resolution | 112 | |
| added value | 47 | |
| address the problem | 120 | |
| adjourn (the session) | 128 | |
| administration | 20,126 | |
| administrative authority | 141 | |
| administrative branch | 126 | |
| administrative guidance | 20 | |
| administrative order | 136 | |
| administrative reforms | 144 | |
| administrative vice minister | 102 | |
| adopt | 131 | |
| adoption | 131 | |
| advance to second | 193 | |
| advanced technology | 150 | |
| advent | 143 | |
| advisory council | 127 | |
| advocate | 158 | |
| affront | 122 | |
| against the stream | 114 | |
| agile | 155 | |
| aging | 159 | |
| aging society | 159 | |
| ahead | 193 | |
| aide | 100 | |
| ailing economy | 15 | |
| akin | 143 | |
| alchemist | 155 | |
| alchemy | 155 | |
| allegation | 141 | |
| allocate | 27,134 | |
| allot | 134 | |
| allow | 182 | |
| alternating current | 152 | |
| amass | 142 | |
| amassment | 142 | |
| amend | 132 | |
| amendment | 132 | |
| ancillary market | 154 | |
| annuity | 37 | |
| annul | 93 | |
| anti-bacterial goods | 161 | |
| (anti-)dumping duty | 48 | |
| anti-inflation policy | 20 | |
| anti-mainstream faction | 107 | |
| antimonopoly law | 50 | |
| antitrust law | 50 | |
| apolitical | 103 | |
| apologize | 123 | |
| appoint ministers | 101 | |
| appreciate | 54 | |
| appreciation | 54 | |
| appropriate | 27 | |
| approval | 130 | |
| approval rate | 102 | |
| approve | 130 | |
| approximately | 63 | |
| apron | 76 | |
| arbitrage | 59 | |
| arithmetic average | 36 | |
| arsenic | 162 | |
| artificial turf | 168 | |
| ascend the throne | 96 | |
| aspersion | 121 | |
| assembly | 127,128 | |
| assume a role | 50 | |
| assume the post of | 101 | |
| Astroturf | 168 | |
| astute | 156 | |
| at random | 91 | |
| at the earliest | 17 | |

| | | |
|---|---|---|
| at the latest | 17 | Bank of Japan | 23 | belt | 76 |
| attach importance to it | | banking industry | 22 | belt-tightening policy | 16 |
| | 120 | bankrolled election | 90 | benchmark price | 18 |
| attach legal identity (to) | | bankruptcy | 31 | bend over backwards | 113 |
| | 28 | barb | 123 | beneficiary | 140 |
| Attorney General | 100 | bare majority | 93 | benevolent | 123 |
| attribute | 114 | bargain (over) | 36 | better | 171 |
| Aum Shinrikyo cult | 162 | bargaining chip | 36 | between | 55 |
| Aum Supreme Truth | 162 | barnstorm | 88 | betweener | 189 |
| autocracy | 97 | barnstorming | 89 | biannual | 29 |
| autograph | 182 | base on balls | 180 | bid | 50 |
| autonomy | 145 | base running | 193 | bid(ding) | 50 |
| avid | 90 | (baseball) field | 168 | bid-rigging | 50 |
| avoid a tag | 194 | baseline | 191 | bidder | 50 |
| award | 165 | bases full | 194 | bidding procedures | 50 |

## B

| | | |
|---|---|---|
| back | 90 | bases-loaded home run | | big shot | 109 |
| back him to the hilt | 90 | | 192 | Big Three brokerage houses | 59 |
| back spread | 29 | bases-loaded walk | 181 | Big Three securities | 59 |
| backer | 90 | batter's box | 185 | bill | 32,129 |
| backfire | 119 | battered wife | 159 | bipartisan | 105 |
| backlash | 117 | batting | 196 | birth rate | 158 |
| backstop | 168 | batting average | 183 | blank | 176 |
| bacteria | 161 | batting eye | 184 | blaspheme | 122 |
| bad bounce | 188 | batting order | 183 | blasphemy | 122 |
| bad condition | 182 | batting practice | 199 | blast | 171,184,190,191 |
| bad control | 180 | batting-practice pitcher | | bleachers | 168 |
| bad hop | 188 | | 175 | bloated bureaucracy | 144 |
| bad loan [debt] | 25 | bean ball | 181 | Blood is thicker than water. | 97 |
| baggy pants | 160 | bear | 65 | |
| bail out | 32,181 | bearish | 65 | bloop | 189 |
| bail(-)out | 32 | bearish factor | 65 | blooper | 189 |
| balance the budget | 133 | beat | 93,169 | blow his horn | 88 |
| balanced budget | 133 | beatout | 189 | blue chip | 60 |
| balk | 182 | become a target of restructuring | | bluster | 116 |
| ballot | 91 | | 34 | Board of Audit | 132 |
| ballot counting | 92 | beeper | 161 | bobble | 198 |
| ballpark | 168 | behemoth | 109 | bolster | 18 |
| Bank of International Settlement [BIS] | 23 | behind-the-scene | 112 | bona fide member | 105 |
| | | belatedly | 56 | bonanza | 106 |

223

| Term | Page |
|---|---|
| bond | 67 |
| bonds to fill a revenue shortfall | 134 |
| bonehead(ed) play | 198 |
| book-closing | 29 |
| boom | 14 |
| boost the economy | 17 |
| boot | 198 |
| boot a grounder | 189 |
| bottom line | 28 |
| bottom of the order | 183 |
| bounce back | 65 |
| bout against Wakanohana | 78 |
| bow dance | 77 |
| bow out | 110 |
| bow twirling ceremony | 77 |
| brain drain | 150 |
| branch manager | 24 |
| breach | 40 |
| breach of contract | 40 |
| breach of trust | 30 |
| Break a leg. | 164 |
| break apart | 108 |
| break even | 28 |
| break-even point | 28 |
| breaking ball | 177 |
| breakthrough | 118 |
| brethren | 106 |
| bribe | 140,141 |
| bribery scandal | 140 |
| bridge bank | 32 |
| bristle | 123 |
| brokerage commission | 59 |
| brokerage (house) | 59 |
| browser | 152 |
| brushback | 181 |
| bubble economy | 14 |
| budget allocation | 134 |
| budget (bill) | 132 |
| Budget Bureau | 132 |
| budget ceiling | 133 |
| budget committee | 127 |
| budget deficit | 133 |
| budget deliberation | 133 |
| Budget message | 129 |
| budget modification | 134 |
| budget reduction | 134 |
| budget surplus | 133 |
| budgetary negotiation | 133 |
| budgetary request | 133 |
| bug | 153 |
| bull | 65 |
| bullet | 187 |
| bullish | 65 |
| bullish factor | 65 |
| bunch | 189 |
| bunt | 186 |
| buoyant | 63 |
| bureaucracy | 144 |
| bureaucrat | 144 |
| burgeoning | 154 |
| burst into a rage | 161 |
| bursting of the bubble economy | 14 |
| business acumen | 156 |
| business bachelor | 158 |
| business conditions | 14 |
| business cycle | 14 |
| business practices | 49 |
| business world | 51 |
| bust | 31 |
| buy | 40 |
| buy order | 60 |
| buyback | 60 |
| buying price | 61 |
| by a great [big, wide] margin | 93 |
| by a small [narrow] margin | 93 |
| by no means | 94 |
| by-election | 85 |
| bystander | 115 |

## C

| Term | Page |
|---|---|
| cabinet | 101 |
| cabinet reshuffle | 101 |
| cajole | 113 |
| call | 128 |
| call the shots | 169 |
| called strike | 177 |
| campaign headquarters | 89 |
| campaign manager | 88 |
| campaign promise | 89 |
| candidate | 87 |
| capital | 67 |
| capital adequacy requirement | 27 |
| capital increase | 67 |
| capital investment | 19 |
| capital reduction | 67 |
| capital tie-up (with) | 39 |
| capitalism | 98 |
| capitalist | 98 |
| Capitol Hill | 128 |
| car ownership rate | 19 |
| career home runs | 192 |
| caretaker government | 98 |
| carom | 197 |
| carry | 130 |
| cash in stock options | 59 |
| cast aspersions on him | 121 |
| cast his ballot | 91 |
| casualty insurance company | 24 |
| catch | 118,196,198 |
| catch fire | 161 |
| catcher's mitt | 195 |

| | | |
|---|---|---|
| caucus | 85 | |
| cause a stir | 116 | |
| cautious | 66 | |
| cave to corporate pressure | 140 | |
| cellar | 170 | |
| Census Bureau | 90 | |
| center-left | 103 | |
| central bank | 23 | |
| centripetal force | 112 | |
| centrism | 103 | |
| centrist | 103 | |
| centrist government | 103 | |
| centrist party | 105 | |
| ceremonial apron | 76 | |
| certified public accountant | 70 | |
| chairman | 105 | |
| chairman of the General Council | 106 | |
| chairman of the (LDP) Diet Affairs Committee | 106 | |
| chairman of the Policy Affairs Research Council | 106 | |
| chamber | 127 | |
| champion | 77 | |
| champion the reforms | 144 | |
| change hands | 40 | |
| chaotic | 66 | |
| charge forward | 78 | |
| cheap labor | 48 | |
| check | 32 | |
| chest protector | 195 | |
| chest-thumping | 116 | |
| chest-thumps | 116 | |
| chief cabinet secretary | 101 | |
| chief policy planner | 106 | |
| child-care leave program | 158 | |
| choke up | 183 | |
| choke up the bat | 186 | |
| chop | 186 | |
| chopper | 186 | |
| churn out | 19 | |
| citizen ombudsman | 143 | |
| city assembly | 128 | |
| city bank | 23 | |
| city hall | 128 | |
| city ordinance | 135 | |
| clash | 64 | |
| clash head-on | 78 | |
| class action by shareholders | 58 | |
| clean the slate | 132 | |
| cleanup batter | 183 | |
| clearing | 25 | |
| cleat | 195 | |
| click (on) | 152 | |
| cling to power | 110 | |
| Clinton administration | 100 | |
| clobber | 169 | |
| close a factory | 39 | |
| close (the session) | 128 | |
| closer | 175 | |
| closing | 128 | |
| closing price | 61 | |
| clout | 109,190 | |
| clutch hitter | 184 | |
| coalition cabinet | 102 | |
| coalition (government) | 102 | |
| code | 154 | |
| collapse | 118 | |
| collapse of the bubble economy | 14 | |
| collateral | 25 | |
| collectible | 26 | |
| collective bargaining | 35 | |
| come from behind | 170 | |
| come into effect | 136 | |
| come into [to] power | 100 | |
| come to a standstill | 134 | |
| come to terms with him | 113 | |
| come to the conclusion | 135 | |
| come to the throne | 96 | |
| come-from-behind victory | 170 | |
| comebacker | 188 | |
| commensurate with | 49 | |
| commercial land | 70 | |
| Commercial Law | 58 | |
| commit an error | 198 | |
| committee | 127 | |
| common law | 135 | |
| common stock | 60 | |
| commonwealth | 97 | |
| communism | 98 | |
| communist | 98 | |
| Communist Party | 105 | |
| commuter marriage | 158 | |
| company official in charge of | 24 | |
| compared to last year | 46 | |
| compensation for (trading) losses | 65 | |
| complete game | 176 | |
| comprehensive tariffication | 46 | |
| (computer) glitch | 153 | |
| computer virus | 153 | |
| concern | 121 | |
| confer | 165 | |

| | | | | | |
|---|---|---|---|---|---|
| confidence vote | 92 | corporate bond | 67 | cripple | 135 |
| Congress | 128 | corporate donation | 89 | criticize | 122 |
| Congressman | 129 | corporate governance | 51 | criticize him by name | 122 |
| connect | 185 | corporate pension | 37 | | |
| connect hitter | 185 | (corporate) racketeer | 58 | cronyism | 102 |
| conservatism | 103 | Corporate Reorganization | | crossroads | 117 |
| conservative | 103 | Law | 31 | crush | 64 |
| consolidate | 144 | corporate society | 51 | crushing defeat | 64,93 |
| consolidated book-closing | | corporate status | 70 | crux of the matter | 120 |
| | 29 | corporate tax | 70 | cul-de-sac | 118 |
| consolidation | 144 | corrective action | 30 | cult | 162 |
| consortium | 39 | corrupt | 142 | cult official(s) | 162 |
| constant | 150 | corrupt and incompetent | | cultist | 162 |
| constituency | 86,90 | | 142 | cultural heritage | 166 |
| constituent | 90 | corruption | 142 | cumulative deficit | 133 |
| constitutional monarchy | | cost cut | 38 | curb | 86 |
| | 96 | cost reduction | 38 | curb costs | 38 |
| constraint | 161 | costly error | 198 | currency market | 54 |
| consumer demand | 18 | costs | 38 | current account | 45 |
| consumer prices | 18 | costs of purchase | 28 | current price | 61 |
| Consumers are perking | | Councillor | 126 | current share price | 61 |
| up. | 19 | count | 179 | curtail inflation | 20 |
| consummate skill | 163 | count the votes | 92 | curve ball | 177 |
| consumption tax | 70 | counter his opinion | 121 | cut a deal | 113 |
| contender | 88 | counterbalance | 116 | cut a figure | 116 |
| contestant | 88 | counterpart | 159 | cut back on costs | 38 |
| contribution | 37 | cover first base | 197 | cut costs [expenses] | 38 |
| control | 46 | cover up | 65,142 | cut red tape | 144 |
| control voluntarily | 47 | cover-up | 65 | cut the Gordian knot | 120 |
| convene | 128 | covert | 142 | cutback(s) in personnel | |
| convention | 85 | coverup | 142 | [staff] | 34 |
| convergence | 145 | cranky | 108 | cutbacks by attrition | 34 |
| convergent | 145 | crash | 64 | cutoff play | 197 |
| convertible bond | 67 | credit | 26 | cybermoney | 154 |
| convey | 152 | credit association | 24 | cycle | 190 |
| conveyor | 152 | credit crunch | 27 | **D** | |
| convocation | 128 | credit union | 24 | daisy clipper | 188 |
| copyright | 151 | credit-rating agency | 27 | darter | 187 |
| copyright system | 151 | creditor | 26 | data processing | 152 |
| coronation | 96 | cringe | 140 | de facto | 105 |

226

| | | |
|---|---|---|
| dead heat | 92 | deliberate | 129 | detract | 122 |
| dead-heat | 92 | deliberation | 129 | detractor | 122 |
| deal on credit | 59 | deliver | 129 | devaluate | 56 |
| deal on margin | 59 | deluge | 150 | devaluation | 56 |
| debacle | 118 | demand | 18 | devalue | 56 |
| debenture (bond) | 67 | demands concerning tax cuts | 72 | developer | 25 |
| debt | 26 | | | devolution | 145 |
| debt-servicing costs | 134 | demarcate the electoral districts | 86 | devolve | 145 |
| debt-serving capability | 26 | | | dicker | 113 |
| | | demarcation | 86 | dictator | 97 |
| debtor | 26 | demeaning | 122 | dictatorship | 97 |
| deceive | 117 | democracy | 98 | diehard hawk | 104 |
| decentralization | 145 | Democrat | 85 | Diet | 126 |
| decentralize | 145 | democratic | 98 | diffusion index [DI] | 14 |
| deceptive | 117 | Democratic Party | 85,105 | dig out | 197 |
| decline | 64,158 | demographic | 91 | dip | 64 |
| decline of land prices | 25 | demography | 91 | direct current | 152 |
| decline of the personal consumption | 18 | denominated in dollars | 67 | direct tax | 70 |
| | | densely-populated | 86 | director general | 101 |
| decode | 154 | deposit-insurance corporation | 31 | dirt | 77 |
| decoration | 165 | | | disapproval | 131 |
| decree | 136 | deposit-insurance system for banks | 31 | disapprove | 131 |
| decry | 122 | | | discharge | 34,101 |
| decrypt | 154 | depreciate | 54 | disciplinary action | 35 |
| decryption | 154 | depreciation | 54,72 | disciplinary dismissal | 35 |
| deduction for dependants | 71 | depression | 15 | disclose the information | 26 |
| | | deputy minister | 102 | | |
| default | 27 | deputy prime minister | 101 | disclosure | 26 |
| defeat | 169 | | | disclosure standards of bad loans | 26 |
| defect | 117 | deputy secretary | 100 | | |
| defector | 117 | deputy secretary general | 105 | discord | 107 |
| defending champion | 163 | | | disgruntled | 102 |
| defense | 196 | derail | 131 | dishonored bill | 32 |
| deficit | 45 | deregulate | 47 | disinflation | 20 |
| deficit-covering bonds | 134 | deregulation | 47 | dismiss | 34 |
| | | derivatives | 67 | dismiss the film | 165 |
| deflation | 20 | derogatory | 123 | dismissal | 34,101 |
| degrading | 122 | designated hitter | 184 | disorder | 134 |
| delete | 152 | despotism | 97 | disparage | 143 |
| deletion | 152 | details | 39 | disparity | 86 |

| | | |
|---|---|---|
| disruption | 108 | |
| dissent | 121 | |
| dissolution | 128 | |
| dissolve | 128 | |
| diuretic | 163 | |
| diversion of funds | 142 | |
| divert | 142 | |
| divest my holdings | 60 | |
| dividend | 63 | |
| diving catch | 196 | |
| division of three powers | 126 | |
| divisive issue(s) | 120 | |
| divorce | 159 | |
| dogged perseverance | 109 | |
| dogma | 104 | |
| doldrums | 15 | |
| dollar-denominated bond | 67 | |
| domestic demand | 18 | |
| domestic violence | 159 | |
| dominant | 107 | |
| dominant power [group] | 107 | |
| donate | 89 | |
| donation | 89 | |
| door-to-door visits | 88 | |
| doping | 163 | |
| doting parent | 159 | |
| double | 190 | |
| double play | 196 | |
| double-figure winner | 176 | |
| dour | 108 | |
| dove | 104 | |
| dovish | 104 | |
| Dow Jones industrial average | 62 | |
| down | 80, 169 | |
| down and away | 178 | |
| down and in | 178 | |
| down-to-earth business | 154 | |
| draft | 32 | |
| draft budget | 133 | |
| drag bunt | 186 | |
| drastic | 34 | |
| drastic action [measures] | 145 | |
| draw a walk | 180 | |
| draw down | 79 | |
| draw (game) | 170 | |
| draw-in | 196 | |
| drive | 187 | |
| drive out | 79 | |
| drop | 64 | |
| drop by 15% | 64 | |
| due process | 132 | |
| dummy company | 30 | |
| dumping | 48 | |
| duster | 181 | |
| duty-free | 71 | |
| dwell (on) | 120 | |
| dwindle | 112 | |
| dynasty | 96 | |
| dystopia | 161 | |
| **E** | | |
| eager | 90 | |
| earn | 176 | |
| earn his 18th save | 175 | |
| earned run | 182 | |
| earned run average [ERA] | 182 | |
| ease the regulations | 47 | |
| easy to catch | 187 | |
| easy-money policy | 16 | |
| eat humble pie | 116 | |
| eating disorders | 162 | |
| economic bubble | 14 | |
| economic chaos | 15 | |
| economic conditions | 14 | |
| economic crisis | 15 | |
| economic friction | 46 | |
| economic growth | 17 | |
| economic recovery | 17 | |
| Economic report | 129 | |
| economic white paper | 14 | |
| economy | 14 | |
| edge (out) | 170 | |
| elderly people living alone | 160 | |
| election | 84 | |
| (election) campaign | 88 | |
| Election Control Commission | 85 | |
| election district | 86 | |
| election irregularities | 86 | |
| election returns | 92 | |
| election system | 84 | |
| electoral district | 86 | |
| electoral system | 84 | |
| electorate | 90 | |
| electric current | 152 | |
| eligibility for election | 84 | |
| eligible voter | 90 | |
| eliminate | 163 | |
| elimination matches | 163 | |
| eliminations | 163 | |
| embezzle | 142 | |
| embezzlement | 142 | |
| embrace | 113 | |
| embroil | 117 | |
| emergency loan | 32 | |
| emerging market | 48 | |
| eminent | 109 | |
| emir | 97 | |
| emirate | 97 | |
| Emperor's Cup | 81 | |
| employees' pension | 37 | |
| enact | 130 | |
| encrypt | 154 | |

| | | | | | |
|---|---|---|---|---|---|
| encryption | 154 | explode | 190 | fat pitch | 179 |
| endorse | 32 | exploratory | 88 | favorite | 87 |
| endorsement | 32,90 | export | 45 | federal government | 97 |
| endorser | 32,90 | export quota | 47 | Federal Reserve Bank | 61 |
| enforce | 136 | export restriction | 47 | Federal Reserve Board | 61 |
| enforcement | 136 | express concern (about) | 121 | federation | 97 |
| Engel's coefficient | 19 | external demand | 18 | feeble government | 98 |
| enhance his clout | 109 | extra-base hit | 190 | feisty | 155 |
| entangle | 134 | extraordinary session | 127 | fetch | 55 |
| entanglement | 134 | exuberant | 108 | fiber optics | 151 |
| entourage | 100 | **F** | | fictitious company | 30 |
| Equal Employment Opportunity Law | 36 | face | 169 | field office bachelor | 158 |
| equal pay for equal work | 36 | face value | 60 | fielding | 196 |
| equity | 27 | face-off | 78 | fielding practice | 199 |
| ergonomics | 150 | facelift | 25 | fight inflation | 20 |
| eureka | 156 | faction | 106 | Fighting Spirit Prize | 81 |
| European Monetary Union [EMU] | 56 | factional strife | 107 | file for bankruptcy protection | 31 |
| evade taxes | 72 | factionalism | 106 | fill me in | 115 |
| exceed | 24,32 | fail | 30 | finals | 163 |
| excess capacity | 19 | fail to catch (a ball) | 198 | finance | 24 |
| excess of debts over assets | 32 | failed Nippon Credit Bank | 30 | financial action | 16 |
| excessive loan [lending] | 24 | failure | 31 | financial combine | 51 |
| exchange market | 54 | fair territory | 168 | financial crunch | 27 |
| exchange rate mechanism | 54 | Fair Trade Commission | 50 | financial industry | 22 |
| exchange risk | 54 | fall | 64 | financial institution | 23 |
| executive order | 136 | fall by its daily maximum limit | 63 | financial instrument | 23 |
| exercise leadership | 112 | fall by the daily trading limit | 63 | financial liberalization | 22 |
| exhibition game | 169 | fall in profits | 28 | financial reforms | 22 |
| exit poll | 91 | fall into disorder | 134 | financial system | 22 |
| expansion | 18 | falsify the book(s) | 29 | financing | 24 |
| expediency | 123 | fan | 177 | fine tuning | 64 |
| expedient | 123 | fastball | 176 | fireball | 177 |
| expenditure | 133 | fastball pitcher | 177 | fireballer | 177 |
| expenses | 38 | fastballer | 177 | fireman | 175 |
| | | fat | 179 | first baseline | 191 |
| | | | | first baseman's glove | 195 |
| | | | | first inning | 170 |
| | | | | first place | 171 |

| | | |
|---|---|---|
| fiscal year | 132 | |
| fiscal action | 16 | |
| fixed costs | 38 | |
| fixed exchange rate system | 54 | |
| (fixed) property tax | 70 | |
| fizzle | 161 | |
| flare up the issue | 121 | |
| flat | 15 | |
| flat tax(ation) | 71 | |
| floating exchange rate system | 54 | |
| fluctuate | 54 | |
| flush | 90 | |
| fly | 187 | |
| fly into a rage | 161 | |
| follow the prearranged procedures | 50 | |
| food expenses | 38 | |
| force down | 79 | |
| force out | 79,194 | |
| forcing out | 79 | |
| foregone conclusion | 135 | |
| foreign exchange market | 54 | |
| foreign exchange rate | 54 | |
| foreign exchange reserve | 54 | |
| foreign relations committee | 127 | |
| forestall | 15 | |
| forfeit | 169 | |
| forfeited game | 169 | |
| forgo 401k plans | 37 | |
| forkball | 177 | |
| formal marriage | 159 | |
| fortitude | 109 | |
| foul | 177 | |
| foul fly | 187 | |
| foul ground | 168 | |
| foul language | 165 |
| foul line | 191 |
| foul play | 141 |
| foul territory | 168 |
| foul tip | 177 |
| four-year tenure | 99 |
| fragment | 159 |
| frame | 170 |
| free trade | 44 |
| freedom of speech | 97 |
| freedom of the press | 97 |
| freewheeling | 44 |
| freeze | 137 |
| fringe candidate | 87 |
| fringe party | 105 |
| from the previous day | 61 |
| front-runner | 87,171 |
| fudge the figures | 34 |
| full of confidence | 183 |
| full-scale model | 150 |
| fumble | 197,198 |
| fund-raise | 89 |
| fund-raiser | 89 |
| fund-raising | 89 |
| fundamentalism | 99 |
| fundamentalist | 99 |
| fungo | 199 |
| future contract | 68 |
| future transactions | 68 |
| **G** | |
| gadget | 150 |
| gain ground | 114 |
| gain the initiative | 112 |
| gainer | 61 |
| gains by its daily maximum limit | 63 |
| gains by the daily trading limit | 63 |
| game-ending home run | 192 |
| game-winning RBI | 192 |
| game-winning run | 193 |
| garbage pitch | 181 |
| garner | 93 |
| GATT | 48 |
| general account | 132 |
| general contractor | 25 |
| general election | 84 |
| general principles | 104 |
| general public | 102 |
| General Secretary | 99 |
| generate | 63 |
| gentrification | 25 |
| gentrify | 25 |
| geriatric problem | 160 |
| geriatrics | 160 |
| germ | 161 |
| get a cut of the action | 63 |
| get back to normal | 135 |
| get his record back to even | 80 |
| get hold of the ball | 186 |
| get hold of the sash | 78 |
| get inside | 79 |
| get the bill shelved | 131 |
| get the cold shoulder | 117 |
| get the upper hand over the enemy | 114 |
| gift tax | 70 |
| Gillet | 181 |
| give a bribe | 141 |
| give the cold shoulder to him | 117 |
| give up | 182 |
| give weight to it | 120 |
| glitterati | 164 |
| glittery life | 164 |
| globe-trotting company | 20 |
| glove work | 196 |

| | | |
|---|---|---|
| gnawing anxiety | 66 | |
| go against the grain | 41 | |
| go bankrupt | 31 | |
| go bust | 31 | |
| go down | 178 | |
| go forward | 78 | |
| go into effect | 136 | |
| go on the rocks | 31 | |
| go on the stump | 88 | |
| go out of business | 31 | |
| go over | 24 | |
| go the distance | 176 | |
| go under | 31 | |
| go-ahead run | 193 | |
| good business conditions | 14 | |
| good condition | 182 | |
| good control | 180 | |
| goose egg | 195 | |
| gopher | 179 | |
| gopher ball | 179 | |
| Gordian knot | 120 | |
| government official | 102 | |
| governor | 23,84 | |
| governor of Tokyo | 84 | |
| grace | 122 | |
| grade | 122 | |
| grand champion | 77 | |
| Grand Old Party [GOP] | 85 | |
| grand slam | 192 | |
| (grand) sumo wrestling | 76 | |
| grass clipper | 188 | |
| grass roots | 88 | |
| gray power | 160 | |
| gridlock | 118 | |
| grip the sash | 78 | |
| gross domestic product [GDP] | 18 | |
| gross national product [GNP] | 18 | |
| ground | 77,188 | |
| ground ball | 188 | |
| ground stand | 168 | |
| ground-rule double | 190 | |
| grounder | 188 | |
| Group of Seven [G7] | 48 | |
| growing expectation | 66 | |
| guarantee | 32 | |
| guaranteed investment contract | 37 | |
| guard the lines | 196 | |
| guard the plate | 186 | |
| gubernatorial election | 84 | |
| guess hitter | 184 | |
| guide the team | 169 | |
| guilt [guilty] by association | 86 | |
| guru | 109 | |

## H

| | | |
|---|---|---|
| hack | 135 | |
| halo | 109 | |
| hamper efforts | 17 | |
| handcuff | 188 | |
| hands down | 169 | |
| hard grounder | 188 | |
| hardliner | 104 | |
| hardship | 31 | |
| harness | 155 | |
| hassle | 121 | |
| have a tug-of-war | 112 | |
| Hawaiian-born | 77 | |
| hawk | 104 | |
| hawkish | 104 | |
| He bit the hand that fed him. | 117 | |
| He is all wet. | 121 | |
| He is of two minds. | 115 | |
| He is prone to injury. | 80 | |
| He keeps a stiff upper lip. | 116 | |
| He knows which side his bread is buttered (on). | 63 | |
| head of state | 98 | |
| head off | 135 | |
| header | 163 | |
| headfirst sliding | 193 | |
| heading | 163 | |
| heartthrob | 164 | |
| heavy favorite | 87 | |
| heavy striker | 184 | |
| hectic (life) | 135 | |
| hedge | 40 | |
| heir apparent | 96 | |
| herald | 118 | |
| herd | 106 | |
| herd instinct | 106 | |
| hidden loss | 28 | |
| hidden profit | 28 | |
| high and inside | 178 | |
| high and outside | 178 | |
| high price | 61 | |
| high-income bracket | 72 | |
| higher echelon | 77 | |
| highest rank wrestler | 77 | |
| highlight | 64 | |
| highly value-added product | 47 | |
| hinder | 44 | |
| hint subtly | 123 | |
| hit a drive | 188 | |
| hit a fly | 187 | |
| hit a liner | 187 | |
| hit bottom | 65 | |
| hit by a pitch | 181 | |
| hit for the cycle | 190 | |
| hit his stride | 183 | |
| hit the corner(s) | 179 | |
| hit the peak | 63 | |

231

| | | |
|---|---|---|
| hit-by-pitch | 181 | |
| Hobson's choice | 115 | |
| hog | 50 | |
| hokum | 122 | |
| hold down inventories [stocks] | 39 | |
| hold down costs | 38 | |
| hold the reins of government | 100 | |
| hold the runner | 182 | |
| hold the sash | 78 | |
| hold top place | 171 | |
| holding company | 58 | |
| hollowing-out of industry | 48 | |
| home health care | 160 | |
| home ownership rate | 19 | |
| home run | 191 | |
| home run producer | 184 | |
| home run slugger | 184 | |
| home-to-home canvas | 88 | |
| homepage | 153 | |
| homer | 191 | |
| honoring program | 165 | |
| hook | 177 | |
| hooligan | 163 | |
| hopeful candidate | 87 | |
| horde | 106 | |
| hot corner | 196 | |
| hot potato | 119 | |
| hotbed | 142 | |
| House of Councillors | 126 | |
| House of Representatives | 126,128 | |
| housing starts | 19 | |
| hover | 55 | |
| hub | 145 | |
| humming economy | 14 | |
| hurt his credit | 143 | |
| hush up | 65 | |

## I

| | | |
|---|---|---|
| I can't hold a candle to him. | 109 | |
| I have an edge over him. | 92 | |
| I have other fish to fry. | 119 | |
| I'll conform to others. | 114 | |
| icon | 152 | |
| idled land | 25 | |
| If the shoe fits, wear it. | 117 | |
| If things don't work out... | 155 | |
| illegal loan [lending] | 24 | |
| immediate effect | 17 | |
| imminent | 118 | |
| impasse | 118 | |
| impeach | 101 | |
| impeachment | 101 | |
| impeccable | 109 | |
| impede | 44 | |
| impending | 118 | |
| imperative | 113 | |
| implement | 136 | |
| implementation | 136 | |
| implicate | 117 | |
| imply | 123 | |
| import | 45 | |
| import restriction | 47 | |
| impresario | 164 | |
| improve the corporate image | 41 | |
| improvement of infrastructure | 19 | |
| impunity | 143 | |
| in a single burst | 79 | |
| in accordance with the law | 58 | |
| in any event [case] | 38 | |

| | | |
|---|---|---|
| in honor of | 100 | |
| in nominal terms | 64 | |
| in one way or another | 38 | |
| in real terms | 64 | |
| in sync | 114 | |
| In the air! | 187 | |
| inactive | 66 | |
| inapt | 49 | |
| inaugurate | 99 | |
| inauguration | 99 | |
| inauguration ceremony | 99 | |
| incentives for newborns | 158 | |
| income | 133 | |
| income statement | 29 | |
| income tax | 70 | |
| increase in profits | 28 | |
| increase its capital | 67 | |
| increase its seats | 94 | |
| incrementalism | 103 | |
| incumbent | 87 | |
| independent | 85 | |
| independent counsel | 101 | |
| independent voters | 85 | |
| indirect tax | 70 | |
| indiscreet | 123 | |
| indiscretion | 123 | |
| industrial hollowing | 48 | |
| inept remark | 123 | |
| inevitability | 41 | |
| inevitable | 31 | |
| infield fly | 187 | |
| infield hit | 189 | |
| infield stand | 168 | |
| influence peddler | 141 | |
| influence peddling | 141 | |
| influential | 107 | |
| informal price-fixing cartel | 50 | |

# 英語索引

| | | |
|---|---|---|
| infringe | 151 | |
| infuse | 119 | |
| infusion | 119 | |
| inherit the throne | 96 | |
| inheritance tax | 70 | |
| initial charge | 78 | |
| initiative | 112 | |
| inject | 27 | |
| injection | 27 | |
| injury time | 163 | |
| inkling | 123 | |
| inning | 170 | |
| innovation | 150 | |
| innovative | 150 | |
| insert | 152 | |
| insertion | 152 | |
| inside grip | 78 | |
| invincible | 20 | |
| inside information | 65 | |
| inside-the-park homer | 191 | |
| insider trading | 65 | |
| insolent | 122 | |
| inspect | 29 | |
| inspection | 29 | |
| institutional investor | 59 | |
| intact | 159 | |
| integrate | 144 | |
| integrated circuit [IC] | 152 | |
| integration | 144 | |
| intellectual property | 151 | |
| intensify | 16 | |
| intentional walk | 180 | |
| interact | 153 | |
| interaction | 153 | |
| interactive | 153 | |
| interdependence | 44 | |
| interdependent | 44 | |
| interest group | 140 | |
| interim government | 98 | |
| interlocking stakes | 60 | |
| interlope | 153 | |
| Internal Revenue Service [IRS] | 70 | |
| International Labor Organization [ILO] | 36 | |
| intervene | 55 | |
| intervention | 55 | |
| intraparty jousting | 107 | |
| intricate | 120 | |
| intrude | 153 | |
| intrusion | 153 | |
| invalid | 92, 136 | |
| investment in plant and equipment | 19 | |
| investment trust [fund] | 68 | |
| investor | 59 | |
| invincible | 20 | |
| invisible trade | 44 | |
| involve | 117 | |
| irregularity | 141 | |
| irreverent | 122 | |
| isometric exercise | 163 | |
| issue | 60, 67, 135 | |
| issue a walk | 180 | |
| It is six and two threes. | 123 | |
| It's out of the question. | 112 | |

## J

| | | |
|---|---|---|
| jack up the price | 18 | |
| jam the batter | 179 | |
| Japan Association of Corporate Executives | 51 | |
| Japan Chamber of Commerce and Industry | 51 | |
| Japan Federation of Economic Organization | 51 | |
| Japan Federation of Employers' Associations | 51 | |
| Japan Sumo Association | 76 | |
| Japanese version of the 401(k) plan | 37 | |
| jerk his jersey off | 163 | |
| joint Diet | 126 | |
| joint responsibility | 143 | |
| joint venture | 39 | |
| judicial branch | 126 | |
| judiciary | 126 | |
| juggernaut | 20 | |
| jump all over the starter | 190 | |
| jump on the bandwagon | 114 | |
| jump to his right | 78 | |
| jumping catch | 196 | |
| Junior Chamber of Commerce | 51 | |
| junior champion | 78 | |
| junior champion second grade | 78 | |
| junior wrestler | 76 | |
| junk bond | 67 | |
| junta | 98 | |
| juvenile prostitution | 162 | |

## K

| | | |
|---|---|---|
| keep a grip on inflation | 20 | |
| keep a low profile | 115 | |
| keep changing | 104 | |
| keep in balance | 45 | |
| Keep it up. | 183 | |
| keep my shirt on | 119 | |
| keep track of bad loans | 26 | |
| keep up with | 150 | |

| | | | | | |
|---|---|---|---|---|---|
| kickback | 141 | leadership election | 105 | limit voluntarily | 47 |
| kingdom | 96 | leading hitter | 183 | line a single | 187 |
| kingpin | 109 | leaping catch | 196 | line his pockets | 142 |
| knee pad | 195 | leave | 186 | linear moter train | 150 |
| knotted game | 170 | left wing | 103 | liner | 187 |
| knuckleball | 177 | left-center (field) | 191 | lingering recession | 15 |
| **L** | | left-handed pitcher | 174 | liquid assets | 27 |
| labor accident | 36 | left-hander | 174 | liquid crystal display | 152 |
| labor costs | 38 | leftist faction | 107 | liquidate | 32 |
| labor dispute | 35 | lefty | 174 | liquidation | 32 |
| labor management | 36 | leg guards | 195 | listed companies | 60 |
| Labor Standards Law | 36 | leg hitter | 193 | listed stock | 60 |
| labor union | 35 | legal identity | 28 | living national treasure | |
| labyrinth | 118 | legalize | 136 | | 166 |
| lack | 94,180 | legislative branch | 126 | load bases | 194 |
| lackluster year | 15 | legislator | 127 | loan | 24 |
| lag | 16 | legislature | 126 | lobby (for) | 140 |
| laissez-fair | 44 | lend | 24 | lobbying | 140 |
| lambast | 165 | lending | 24 | lobbyist | 140 |
| lame duck | 102 | lending guidelines | 24 | local area network | |
| land price | 25 | less children | 158 | [LAN] | 153 |
| land price tax | 70 | letter high | 181 | local assembly | 127 |
| land shark | 25 | level off | 25,159 | local elections | 84 |
| landslide victory | 93 | level-headed | 103 | local government | 145 |
| laptop computer | 151 | lever out | 79 | local tax | 70 |
| large-scale retail stores | | liberal | 103 | lofty goal | 104 |
| law | 50 | Liberal Democratic Party | | logrolling | 140 |
| large-scale tax cut | 72 | [LDP] | 105 | loincloth | 76 |
| latest numbers [figures] | | liberalism | 103 | long hit | 190 |
| | 62 | liberalist | 103 | long-distance marriage | |
| laureate | 165 | liberalization | 48 | | 158 |
| lavish spending | 19 | liberalize | 48 | long-term credit bank | 23 |
| law maker | 127 | libertarian | 103 | longball hitter | 184 |
| laws restricting the | | licensed tax accountant | | longer life spans | 160 |
| opening of big new | | | 70 | look on | 115 |
| stores | 50 | life insurance company | | loophole | 73 |
| lay the groundwork for it | | | 24 | loosen the regulations | |
| | 112 | lift out | 79 | | 47 |
| lead off | 183 | limit on the amount of | | lopsided | 49 |
| leader | 105 | loans | 24 | lose | 93,130,169 |

234

| | | |
|---|---|---|
| lose (a bout) by default 80 | make it illegal 136 | member of the lower house 126 |
| lose a seat 93 | make it ineffective 136 | member of the upper house 126 |
| lose public confidence 30 | make it legal 136 | |
| lose self-control 161 | make money hand over fist 63 | memorial 162 |
| lose the initiative 112 | | memorial service 162 |
| loser 61 | make-or-break bet 59 | merge (with) 40 |
| losing pitcher 175 | makeover 89 | merger 39 |
| loss 65 | malevolent 123 | merger and acquisition [M&A] 40 |
| loss by default 80 | malpractice 141 | |
| lousy film 164 | manage to stabilize the financial system 22 | megamerger 40 |
| low and inside 178 | | merry-go-round 181 |
| low and outside 178 | management-labor dispute 35 | mesmerize kids 164 |
| low fertility 158 | | Metropolitan Assembly 128 |
| low price 61 | management-labor relations 35 | |
| low-income bracket 72 | | middle 178 |
| Lower and Upper Houses 126 | margin 93 | middle-income bracket 72 |
| | market economy 44 | |
| lower echelon 77 | market opening 48 | middle-reliever 175 |
| Lower House 126,129 | market price 61 | midterm election 85 |
| ludicrous 123 | marriage without love 159 | milestone 119 |
| lull 66 | | military regime 97 |
| **M** | mask 195 | millennium bug 153 |
| | mass consumption 19 | mini-party 105 |
| maegashira No.1 78 | mass production 19 | minimum tax rate 71 |
| magnet 109 | masses 102 | minister 101 |
| magnetic levitation train 150 | massive impact 150 | minister without portfolio 102 |
| | match 78 | |
| mainstream faction 107 | materialistic society 161 | ministries and agencies 144 |
| maintain 17 | maul 165 | |
| major 59 | maverick 116 | minor adjustment 64 |
| majority 93 | maximum tax rate 71 | misconduct 141 |
| make a catch 196 | mayor 84 | misdeed 141 |
| make a deal 113 | meat-and-potatoes issue 119 | misgivings 121,141 |
| make a killing 63 | | mistrust in politics 107 |
| make a mountain out of a molehill 108 | medal 165 | moderate 103 |
| | Medicaid 37 | modification 134 |
| make a petition 140 | medical expenses 38 | modify 134 |
| make a ripple effect 17 | Medicare 37 | mogul 109 |
| make a splash 116 | megamerger 40 | momentous phase 118 |
| make an error 198 | member of the Diet 126 | momentous stage 118 |

235

| | | | | | |
|---|---|---|---|---|---|
| monarch | 96 | national census | 90 | nominate | 88 |
| monarchy | 96 | national consensus | 132 | nomination | 88 |
| monolith | 106 | national flag | 98 | nominee | 88 |
| monolithic | 106 | national pension | 37 | Nomura Securities | 59 |
| monopolize | 50 | (national) referendum | | non-approval rate | 102 |
| monument | 162 | | 84 | non-bank (financial institution) | 23 |
| more likely (to) | 159 | National Tax Administration Agency | | | |
| moribund | 98 | | 70 | non-mainstream faction | 107 |
| mortgage | 25 | | | | |
| Mother's Body Protection Law | 158 | nationalism | 99 | non-profit organization | 51 |
| | | nationalist | 99 | | |
| motion | 129,130 | natural gas | 47 | non-tariff barrier | 46 |
| mount the throne | 96 | natural resources | 47 | nonconfidence motion | 135 |
| move forward | 78 | naysayer | 121 | | |
| move into first place | 171 | necessary expenses | 38 | nonconfidence vote | 92 |
| move within a small range | 55 | neck and neck with him | 92 | nonpartisan | 85 |
| | | | | nonperforming loan | 25 |
| much ado about nothing | 108 | negative growth | 17 | nonpolitical | 103 |
| | | negotiate | 133 | nose-dive | 64 |
| muck | 142 | nepotism | 143 | notch | 176 |
| muckrake | 142 | nerve gas | 162 | notify | 136 |
| muff | 198 | net earnings | 28 | novelty | 150 |
| multi-seat constituency | 86 | net (business) profit | 28 | now defunct | 31 |
| | | neutral | 103 | Now that you are my friend... | 113 |
| multinational company | 20 | neutralism | 103 | | |
| | | neutrality | 103 | nuclear family | 159 |
| municipal government | 145 | New York Stock Exchange | 61 | (null and) void | 136 |
| | | | | nullification | 93 |
| muscle out | 79 | newcomer | 87 | nullify | 93 |
| muse | 120 | next of kin | 143 | nursery home | 160 |
| mutual fund | 68 | nibble | 179 | nursery school teacher | 158 |
| **N** | | niche | 154 | | |
| nab a superstar | 164 | night game | 169 | nursery school without licence | 158 |
| nail | 194 | Nikkei stock average | 62 | | |
| narrowly | 130 | nimble | 155 | nursing care system | 160 |
| NASDAQ composite index | 62 | nitty-gritty | 120 | **O** | |
| | | no run | 195 | oath | 99 |
| nasty ground ball | 189 | no-hit-no-run | 176 | oblique mention | 123 |
| national anthem | 98 | no-hitter | 176 | obliterate | 117 |
| national budget | 132 | Nobel laureate | 165 | off-field hit | 184 |

| | | |
|---|---|---|
| off-putting | 122 | |
| off-season | 168 | |
| off-the-book | 30 | |
| offense | 196 | |
| offer a bribe | 141 | |
| official announcement | 136 | |
| official discount rate | 16 | |
| officious | 108 | |
| offset | 26 | |
| offset debts against credits | 26 | |
| oil crisis | 47 | |
| old people living alone | 160 | |
| old-age pension | 37 | |
| omission | 137 | |
| on a full count | 180 | |
| on a year-on-year basis | 46 | |
| on average | 62 | |
| on the fists | 179 | |
| on (the) grounds of | 34 | |
| on the platform | 89 | |
| on-base percentage | 193 | |
| on-deck (batter's) circle | 185 | |
| one-cushion shot | 197 | |
| One thing leads to another. | 155 | |
| ongoing | 130 | |
| onlooker | 115 | |
| open bid(ding) | 50 | |
| open (the session) | 128 | |
| open trade | 44 | |
| opening | 128 | |
| opening price | 61 | |
| operating funds | 27 | |
| operating system [OS] | 152 | |
| opponent | 88 |
| opposite-field hit | 184 |
| opposition party | 104 |
| ordeal | 31 |
| order | 60,165 |
| Order of Cultural Merit | 165 |
| ordinance | 135 |
| ordinary session | 127 |
| organization advocating women's right | 158 |
| organize a cabinet | 101 |
| oust | 117 |
| out of sync | 114 |
| out pitch | 178 |
| outcome | 94 |
| outcry | 135 |
| outfield stand | 168 |
| outnumber | 108 |
| outpace | 151 |
| outpitch | 180 |
| outside grip | 78 |
| outside leg trip | 79 |
| outsource | 39 |
| outsourcing | 39 |
| outspend the opponent | 90 |
| outstanding balance | 28 |
| outstanding bond | 67 |
| Outstanding Performance Prize | 81 |
| outstanding shares | 58 |
| outwit | 117 |
| Oval Office | 100 |
| over-the-counter stock | 60 |
| overarm throw | 79 |
| overcapacity | 19 |
| overdue | 26 |
| overhanded pitcher | 174 |
| overheat | 14 |
| override | 131 |
| overriding human rights | 131 |
| overriding problem | 131 |
| oversee the budget | 132 |
| overstaffing problem | 34 |
| oversupply | 18 |
| overt | 142 |
| overthrow | 181 |
| own goal | 163 |
| owner | 25 |

## P

| | |
|---|---|
| package | 129 |
| pad | 133 |
| padded bill | 133 |
| padded request | 133 |
| padding | 133 |
| pager | 161 |
| painstaking | 109 |
| paint the corner(s) | 179 |
| pan | 165 |
| panel | 127 |
| paradigm | 119 |
| parallel | 152 |
| parallel import | 44 |
| paralyze | 135 |
| paramount | 109 |
| Parliament | 126 |
| Parliamentary Affairs Chairman | 106 |
| partial opening of the rice market | 48 |
| partnership | 39 |
| party in power | 104 |
| party-backed candidate | 87 |
| party-endorsed candidate | 87 |
| party-recommended candidate | 87 |

| Term | Page |
|---|---|
| party-supported candidate | 87 |
| partyism | 104 |
| pass a bill | 130 |
| passage | 130 |
| passed ball | 181 |
| patent | 151 |
| patent infringement | 151 |
| patience | 123 |
| patriarch | 108 |
| patriarchy | 108 |
| pave the way | 44 |
| pay | 160 |
| pay homage [tribute] to his predecessor | 99 |
| pay off | 141 |
| payoff | 140 |
| payout | 37 |
| peg | 195 |
| pejorative | 123 |
| pending | 131 |
| pending question | 131 |
| penetrate | 153 |
| penetration | 153 |
| pennant race | 171 |
| pension funds | 37 |
| pensive | 120 |
| people's life indicators | 14 |
| pep rally | 89 |
| pep talk | 89 |
| pepper (game) | 199 |
| per annum | 29 |
| per capita | 29 |
| per diem | 29 |
| perfect game | 176 |
| peripheral equipment | 152 |
| perks | 39 |
| permanent tax cut | 72 |
| person in charge of | 24 |
| personal consumption | 18 |
| personal spending | 18 |
| personnel costs | 38 |
| pervade | 161 |
| pervasive | 161 |
| pessimism prevails | 66 |
| petition | 140 |
| phase out | 26 |
| philanthropy | 41 |
| pick off the runner | 182 |
| pick up his endorsement | 90 |
| pick up his 18th save | 175 |
| pick up his 7th win | 176 |
| pick-off throw | 182 |
| picket | 36 |
| piracy | 151 |
| pirate | 151 |
| pirate(d) edition | 151 |
| pitch a complete game | 176 |
| pitch a perfect game | 176 |
| pitch himself | 88 |
| pitching staff | 174 |
| pitfall | 118 |
| pivot | 107 |
| pivotal | 107 |
| place priority on it | 120 |
| placement office for senior citizens | 160 |
| planned economy | 44 |
| plant and equipment investment | 19 |
| platform | 104 |
| play catch | 198 |
| play center field | 196 |
| play dumb | 113 |
| play first base | 196 |
| play possum | 113 |
| plebiscite | 84 |
| pledge | 89 |
| plenary session | 127 |
| plug the (loop) holes | 73 |
| plummet | 64 |
| plunge | 64 |
| plutocracy | 106 |
| plutocrat | 106 |
| polarization | 44 |
| polarize | 44 |
| policy maker | 127 |
| policy reversal | 56 |
| political donations by companies | 89 |
| (political) novice | 87 |
| political party | 104 |
| political skills | 112 |
| poll | 91 |
| pollster | 91 |
| pop fly | 187 |
| pop-up | 187 |
| populace | 102 |
| popularity | 161 |
| population inflow | 86 |
| population outflow | 86 |
| pork (barrel) | 141 |
| portal (site) | 153 |
| portfolio | 68,102 |
| positive growth | 17 |
| possible loss of jobs | 35 |
| possible weakness | 66 |
| post a record surplus | 45 |
| posted price | 50 |
| postulate | 150 |
| potentate | 108 |
| potential | 155 |
| power hitter | 184 |
| power struggle | 112 |
| powerful throw | 197 |
| powerhouse | 107 |
| practice | 198 |

| | | |
|---|---|---|
| pre-election campaign 88 | profanity 122 | pull out of the tournament 80 |
| precipitate 23 | professional ethics 30 | pulpit 89 |
| precipitation 23 | proficiency 153 | punitive tariff 46 |
| predict 45 | proficient 153 | puppet regime 98 |
| predominant 107 | proficient in English 153 | purification 77,143 |
| prefectural assembly 128 | profit and loss statement [P/L] 29 | purify 77 |
| prefectural ordinance 135 | | purpose pitch 181 |
| preferred stock 60 | progressive tax(ation) 71 | push down 79 |
| prequel 164 | progressive tax(ation) system 71 | push out 79 |
| President 99 | | put a tax (on) 71 |
| president 23,105 | promiscuous 162 | put him out 194 |
| presidential decree 136 | promising market 154 | put it into effect 136 |
| presidential election 84 | promissory note 32 | put it on hold 131 |
| presidential prerogative 101 | promoter 164 | put restrictions (on) 47 |
| | promulgate 136 | put the bill to a vote 130 |
| press secretary 100 | promulgation 136 | put-up game 169 |
| press the bank 30 | prop up 160 | **Q** |
| pressing issue 119 | proportional representation system 86 | quantum jump 155 |
| pressure group 140 | | quantum leap 155 |
| presume 68 | proprietor 25 | quest 150 |
| presumption 68 | protect the plate 186 | questionary 91 |
| pretax losses 28 | protection of privacy 154 | questionnaire 91 |
| pretax profits 28 | protectionism 44 | quibble 40 |
| pretentious 122 | protectionist 44 | quick hook 175 |
| prevail 161 | provide tax breaks 72 | **R** |
| prevalent 161 | provision 136 | rack up 93 |
| prevent imports 44 | provisional budget 98,134 | radical 103 |
| price-earnings ratio 63 | provisional government 98 | raison d'être 112 |
| primary 84 | | rake-off 141 |
| prime minister 101 | pry the market open 48 | rally 65 |
| prime rate 29 | public confidence 30 | ram 130 |
| private company 20 | public corporation 19 | random sampling 91 |
| private sector investment 19 | public fund [money] 27 | ranking list 77 |
| | public investment 19 | rap out 190 |
| privatization 20 | Public Offices Election Law 85 | rapidly growing market 48 |
| privatize 20 | | |
| privy (to) 114 | public works 19 | ratio of job offers to job-seekers 35 |
| proclaim 136 | pull hitter 185 | |
| proclamation 136 | pull off 78 | |
| profane 122 | | |

| | | | | | |
|---|---|---|---|---|---|
| ratio of the stock holdings | 60 | regional autonomy | 145 | resolution | 130 |
| rationalization | 39 | regional bank | 23 | resolution and collection bank | 32 |
| rationalize | 39 | regulate | 46 | resolve | 130 |
| raw materials | 47 | regulation | 46 | respectively | 45 |
| real estate | 25 | rehearse a speech | 89 | respondent | 91 |
| realtor | 25 | reimburse | 67 | restoration of historical assets | 166 |
| rebound | 65 | reinforce | 16 | restriction | 46 |
| rebuff | 116 | reject | 131 | restructure plan | 32 |
| recap | 120 | rejection | 131 | restructuring | 34 |
| recapitulate | 120 | rejuvenate | 108 | result | 114 |
| recapitulation | 120 | relativism | 97 | result (from) | 16 |
| receiver | 31 | relax the regulations | 47 | resume | 128 |
| recess | 128 | relaxation | 47 | resumption | 128 |
| recession | 15 | relay | 197 | retail prices | 18 |
| recipient | 27 | relief pitcher | 174 | retained earnings | 28 |
| reciprocal trade | 44 | reliever | 174 | retaliatory tariff | 46 |
| reciprocity | 44 | relinquish their reign | 170 | retire the side | 182 |
| reconcile the book(s) | 30 | relocation | 145 | retrieve | 26 |
| record high | 35 | relocation of the capital | 145 | return to normal | 135 |
| recover | 17 | | | return to power | 100 |
| recovery | 18 | reluctant | 27 | returns | 63 |
| red tape | 144 | remain neutral | 103 | revaluate | 56 |
| redemption | 67 | remit | 27 | revaluation | 56 |
| redenomination (downward) | 67 | remittance | 27 | revalue | 56 |
| | | removal | 101 | reveal | 39 |
| reduce budget | 134 | Republican | 85 | revenue | 133 |
| reduce its capital | 67 | repeal | 136,137 | review | 37,134 |
| reduction in profits | 28 | Representative | 126,129 | revise | 58,132 |
| redundancy | 34 | reprimand | 35 | revision of the Commercial Law | 58 |
| redundant | 34 | reproach | 122 | | |
| redundant workers | 34 | republic | 96 | revision of the Constitution | 132 |
| referee | 77 | Republican Party | 85 | | |
| reformist party | 105 | rescind | 136 | revive | 108 |
| refute | 121 | rescindment | 137 | revocation | 137 |
| regain | 30 | rescue scheme [plan] | 32 | revoke | 136 |
| regain the upper hand | 114 | residence tax | 70 | rhetoric | 123 |
| | | residential land | 70 | rifle a single | 187 |
| regal | 96 | resolute | 130 | rig market prices | 51 |
| regal power | 96 | resolute action [measures] | 145 | | |

| | | |
|---|---|---|
| right to stand for office | 84 | |
| right to vote | 84 | |
| right wing | 103 | |
| right-center (field) | 191 | |
| right-handed pitcher | 174 | |
| right-hander | 174 | |
| righteous | 143 | |
| rightist faction | 107 | |
| ring | 76 | |
| ring entering ceremony | 76 | |
| ripple effect | 17 | |
| rise | 62 | |
| risk-averse society | 66 | |
| robust | 14 | |
| romp | 170 | |
| root cause | 16 | |
| root out corporate racketeers | 58 | |
| routine fly | 187 | |
| ruler | 97 | |
| ruling party [power] | 104 | |
| rumblings | 102 | |
| run a dead heat | 92 | |
| run and hit | 186 | |
| run down | 195 | |
| run for the presidency | 87 | |
| run the gauntlet | 31 | |
| run(s) batted in [RBI] | 192 | |
| run-of-the-mill film | 164 | |
| run-scoring hit | 189 | |
| runner | 193 | |
| runner-up | 87 | |
| runners at the corners | 185 | |
| running mate | 88 | |
| runoff (vote election) | 93 | |

## S

| | | |
|---|---|---|
| sacrifice | 187 | |
| safeguard | 64 | |
| saga | 165 | |
| sale on credit | 59 | |
| sales tax | 70 | |
| sanitize | 143 | |
| sarin attack in the subway (system) | 162 | |
| sash | 76 | |
| save on expenses | 38 | |
| savior | 143 | |
| scandal | 141 | |
| scatter | 182 | |
| schmuck | 87 | |
| scoop up | 63 | |
| scratch hit | 189 | |
| screen | 164 | |
| screening | 164 | |
| screenplay | 164 | |
| screwball | 177 | |
| scrounge | 102 | |
| seam | 196 | |
| search engine | 153 | |
| second-highest rank wrestler | 77 | |
| second-tier | 59 | |
| secretary | 100 | |
| secretary general | 105 | |
| Secretary of State | 100 | |
| secure 50 seats | 94 | |
| securities | 60 | |
| Securities and Exchange Commission [SEC] | 58 | |
| Securities and Exchange Law | 58 | |
| securities firm [company, house] | 59 | |
| securitization | 68 | |
| securitize | 68 | |

| | | |
|---|---|---|
| selected stock [issue] | 60 | |
| selective hitter | 184 | |
| self-imposed control | 47 | |
| sell order | 60 | |
| selling price | 61 | |
| semi-finals | 163 | |
| semiconductor | 152 | |
| seminal start-up | 155 | |
| Senate | 129 | |
| Senator | 129 | |
| senior official | 102 | |
| senior statesman | 108 | |
| senior wrestler | 76 | |
| separate | 144 | |
| separate surnames for married couples | 159 | |
| separate taxation | 71 | |
| separation | 144 | |
| separation of three powers | 126 | |
| sequel | 164 | |
| series | 152 | |
| serve four terms | 127 | |
| session | 127 | |
| set a limit on the amount of loans | 24 | |
| sex-related industry | 162 | |
| sexual harassment | 36 | |
| shake off a sign | 182 | |
| shake-up | 39 | |
| sham | 122 | |
| share | 58 | |
| share broker | 59 | |
| shareholder | 58 | |
| shareholders' meeting | 58 | |
| shatter | 161 | |
| sheer | 122 | |
| shelf the bill | 131 | |
| shift to a republic | 96 | |
| shin guards | 195 | |

241

| | | | | | |
|---|---|---|---|---|---|
| shoestring catch | 197 | slugfest | 190 | spectacular | 165 |
| shoo-in | 87 | slugger | 184 | speculate | 59 |
| shoot up | 62 | slugging average | 190 | speculation | 59 |
| shootout | 163 | sluggish auto sales | 15 | Speculation is swirling. | 115 |
| short hop | 197 | slump | 15 | speculative | 59 |
| shortage of day-care centers | 158 | slush fund | 142 | speculator | 59 |
| shoulder | 26 | smarts | 184 | speed financial reforms | 22 |
| showdown | 107 | smash | 184 | speedster | 193 |
| shrink | 64 | smoke | 177 | spending | 133 |
| shut down a factory | 39 | snap election | 84 | spending irregularity | 141 |
| shut out | 176 | snare the sash | 78 | spin off | 40 |
| shutout | 176 | snatch a superstar | 164 | spin-off | 40 |
| sidearmed pitcher | 174 | sneak preview | 165 | spiral | 62 |
| signature | 182 | soar | 62 | split | 108 |
| simplify | 144 | soccer lottery | 163 | spot pitcher | 179 |
| single mother | 158 | (social and) entertainment expenses | 38 | spot reliever | 174 |
| single (hit) | 189 | social convention | 161 | sprawl | 145 |
| single-seat constituency (system) | 86 | Social Democratic Party | 105 | spray hitter | 184 |
| sit back | 115 | social hub | 145 | spring labor offensive | 35 |
| sitting | 87 | social norms | 143 | spring training | 168 |
| six straight wins [victories] | 80 | socialism | 99 | springboard | 114 |
| skeptical | 115 | socialist | 99 | squabble | 121 |
| skepticism | 115 | solicit the amendment | 132 | squat | 78 |
| skim money | 24 | solicitation | 132 | squeeze | 186 |
| skirt the media | 165 | solidarity | 35 | stability | 22 |
| skunk works | 150 | solo homer | 191 | stabilization | 22 |
| skyrocket | 62 | someone inside | 65 | stabilize | 22 |
| slam | 165,184 | sound | 26 | stable | 76 |
| slap | 78 | soundness | 26 | (stable) master | 76 |
| slap down | 79 | soured on | 66 | stablemate | 76 |
| slash costs | 38 | southpaw | 174 | stadium | 168 |
| slate of candidates | 88 | sovereignty | 98 | stagflation | 20 |
| slide | 64 | spearhead | 112 | staggering accomplishment | 109 |
| slider | 177 | special interest legislator | 140 | staggering achievement | 109 |
| slightly lower | 55 | | | stagnant | 15 |
| slob fashion | 160 | | | | |
| slug | 184,190 | special session | 127 | stagnation | 15 |

| | | |
|---|---|---|
| stake | 117 | |
| stall | 134 | |
| stamp out corruption | 143 | |
| stand by | 115 | |
| stand put | 16 | |
| stand-up double | 190 | |
| standstill | 134 | |
| start | 78 | |
| start-up | 155 | |
| starter | 174 | |
| starting pitcher | 174 | |
| state of the Union message | 129 | |
| state-of-the-art technology | 150 | |
| state-owned company | 20 | |
| state-run company | 20 | |
| static electricity | 152 | |
| statute law | 135 | |
| statutory law | 135 | |
| stay afloat | 31 | |
| stay put | 16 | |
| steal | 193 | |
| steal home | 193 | |
| steer clear of controversy | 121 | |
| stem | 114 | |
| stem (from) | 16 | |
| step out of the ring | 79 | |
| step up to the plate | 185 | |
| stimulate the economy | 17 | |
| stipulate | 40 | |
| stipulation | 40 | |
| stock | 58 | |
| stock broker | 59 | |
| stock market | 61 | |
| stock market crash | 64 | |
| stock name | 60 | |
| stock option | 59 | |
| stock price | 61 |
| stockholder | 58 |
| stockholders' meeting | 58 |
| stolen bases [SB] | 193 |
| stop tax evasion | 73 |
| stopper | 175 |
| storm in a teacup | 108 |
| straightjacket | 161 |
| straight wins | 169 |
| straitjacket | 161 |
| straits | 118 |
| strand | 186 |
| straw bales | 77 |
| straw ridge | 76 |
| stream | 114 |
| streamline | 39 |
| streamlining | 39 |
| strenuous | 108 |
| stress | 89 |
| strike | 177 |
| strike down | 136 |
| strike out | 177,178 |
| strikeout | 177 |
| strikeout pitch | 178 |
| strip him of his elected post | 93 |
| strong arm | 197 |
| strong candidate | 87 |
| strong yen | 54 |
| structural factors | 46 |
| Structural Impediments Initiative Talks | 49 |
| structural recession | 15 |
| stuck in a rut | 110 |
| stymie | 162 |
| subcommittee | 127 |
| sublime idea [philosophy] | 104 |
| submission | 129 |
| submit a bill | 129 |
| subordinated loan | 29 |
| subsidize | 140 |
| subsidy | 140 |
| subsist on welfare | 160 |
| succeed to the throne | 96 |
| succession to the throne | 96 |
| succumb to the enemy | 117 |
| suffer | 36 |
| suffer a loss | 169 |
| suffer a second loss | 80 |
| suffer from | 30 |
| suffer two losses | 80 |
| (sumo) wrestler | 76 |
| Super 301 Article | 49 |
| superlative | 109 |
| supersede him | 143 |
| supplementary budget | 134 |
| supply | 18 |
| support | 90 |
| supporter | 90 |
| sure-handed infield | 196 |
| surge | 62 |
| surpass | 32 |
| surplus | 45 |
| surplus in labor force | 34 |
| survivor's pension | 37 |
| survivorship | 37 |
| suspend | 131 |
| suspended | 169 |
| suspension | 131 |
| suspension | 169 |
| suspicion | 141 |
| sustainable growth | 18 |
| swamp computers | 154 |
| swat | 190 |
| swear | 99 |
| sweeping victory | 93 |

| | | |
|---|---|---|
| sweet spot | 186 | |
| swing from the heels | 186 | |
| swinging strike | 177 | |
| swipe | 154 | |
| swipe | 193 | |
| swipe machine | 154 | |
| synergy | 17 | |

## T

| | | |
|---|---|---|
| table the bill | 131 |
| tag out | 194 |
| tag up | 194 |
| tagging up | 194 |
| take a bath | 65 |
| take a bribe | 141 |
| take a concerted [joint] step | 56 |
| take a page from him | 109 |
| take a pitch | 178 |
| take a (sharp) dive | 64 |
| take action | 17 |
| take effect | 136 |
| take it into effect | 136 |
| take measures to stimulate the economy | 17 |
| take on him | 119 |
| take on immense importance | 119 |
| take on the burdens | 119 |
| take over | 40 |
| take over the reins of government | 100 |
| take part in volunteer activities | 41 |
| take preventive measures against racketeer | 58 |
| takeover | 40 |
| takeover bid [TOB] | 40 |
| tally | 92 |
| tally up the election returns | 92 |
| tangle | 134 |
| taper off | 27 |
| tariff barrier | 46 |
| tariffication | 46 |
| tarnish | 122 |
| tarnished | 122 |
| tax break | 72 |
| tax burden | 70 |
| tax collection | 71 |
| Tax Commission | 72 |
| tax credit | 71 |
| tax cut | 72 |
| tax deduction | 71 |
| tax evasion | 72 |
| tax haven | 73 |
| tax hike | 72 |
| tax increase | 72 |
| Tax is high. | 71 |
| Tax is low. | 71 |
| tax (on) | 71 |
| tax payer | 70 |
| tax raise | 72 |
| tax rate | 71 |
| tax return | 70 |
| tax revenue | 71 |
| Tax (System Research) Council | 72 |
| tax-exempt | 71 |
| tax-free | 71 |
| taxation | 71 |
| taxation at the source | 71 |
| taxation reform | 72 |
| technically proficient | 153 |
| Technique Prize | 81 |
| technology transfer | 151 |
| temporary factors | 46 |
| tenacious entrepreneur | 155 |
| tenancy | 77 |
| tenet | 104 |
| tentative plan | 132 |
| test the waters | 115 |
| Texas leaguer | 189 |
| Texas leaguer's hit | 189 |
| That will be the case. | 155 |
| That's the way it goes. | 119 |
| the Bank of Japan's quarterly survey | 14 |
| the Federation of Malaysia | 97 |
| the instant they made contact | 78 |
| The market has been saturated. | 15 |
| the other way around | 40 |
| the right field line | 190 |
| The shoe is on the other foot. | 118 |
| The situation got tough. | 118 |
| the Soviet Union | 97 |
| The table is set. | 185 |
| The tables are turned. | 118,170 |
| the (British) Commonwealth of Nations | 97 |
| There are plenty more fish in the sea. | 119 |
| third base coach | 194 |
| third baseline | 191 |
| third-highest rank wrestler | 78 |
| three-bagger | 190 |
| three-base (hit) | 190 |
| three-run homer | 191 |
| throne | 96 |
| throng | 106 |

| | | | | | |
|---|---|---|---|---|---|
| throw him to the dirt | 79 | trading company [house] | | two-base (hit) | 190 |
| throw the book at him | | | 46 | two-digit inflation | 20 |
| | 143 | trailblazer | 150 | two-run-scoring hit | 189 |
| throw to the plate | 197 | training | 198 | tyranny | 97 |
| thrust forward | 78 | transient | 100 | **U** | |
| tie | 170 | transfer technology (to | | ubiquitous | 161 |
| tie (game) | 170 | China) | 151 | ultraleft | 103 |
| tie up | 39 | transition | 100 | unaffiliated voters | 85 |
| tie-breaker | 81 | transmission | 152 | unarmed neutrality | 103 |
| tie-up | 39 | transmit | 152 | uncollectible | 26 |
| tiebreaking home run | 192 | transparency | 26 | unconfirmed information | |
| tight | 134 | transportation expenses | | | 65 |
| tighten | 16 | | 38 | underarm throw | 79 |
| tight-money policy | 16 | travel expenses | 38 | underarmed pitcher | 174 |
| timely hit | 189 | treacherous | 117 | underfinanced | 90 |
| tirade | 122 | treachery | 117 | underhanded pitcher | 174 |
| titan | 109 | trespass | 154 | undermine | 122 |
| Tokyo Stock Exchange | | trigger | 64 | underpopulated | 86 |
| | 61 | triple | 190 | understate its employ- | |
| toot his horn | 88 | Triple Crown | 183 | ment | 34 |
| top 50 sumo wrestlers | 77 | triple play | 196 | unearned run | 182 |
| top of the order | 183 | trust bank | 23 | unemployment rate | 35 |
| top slot | 171 | trustworthy | 107 | unfair | 49 |
| TOPIX [Tokyo Stock | | try to throw (down) | 79 | unheard-of | 118 |
| Price Index] | 62 | tub thumper | 89 | union | 97 |
| topknot | 76 | tug-of-war | 112 | universal suffrage | 84 |
| torrent | 114 | tumble | 64 | unlisted stock | 60 |
| toss him to the dirt | 79 | turf | 144 | unprecedented | 118 |
| totalitarian | 99 | turf battle | 144 | unseat him | 143 |
| totalitarianism | 99 | turn around a fastball | | unsuitable | 49 |
| tournament | 77 | | 186 | untrustworthy | 107 |
| tout his idea | 121 | turn around Japan's | | up 40 percent from a | |
| town assembly | 128 | politics | 118 | year earlier | 46 |
| trade | 55 | turn face about | 170 | up and away | 178 |
| trade balance | 45 | turn the tables [tide] | | up and in | 178 |
| trade barrier | 46 | | 170 | Upper House | 126 |
| trade deficit | 45 | turnout | 91 | upsurge | 62 |
| trade friction | 46 | turnover | 61 | upturn of the economy | 17 |
| trade imbalance | 45 | turnover (rate) | 35 | URL [Uniform Resource | |
| trade surplus | 45 | two-bagger | 190 | Locator] | 153 |

| Term | Page |
|---|---|
| Uruguay round | 48 |
| U.S. Treasury bond | 67 |
| usurp | 142 |
| usurpation | 142 |
| utopia | 161 |

## V

| Term | Page |
|---|---|
| valid | 92 |
| vanguard | 104 |
| vapid | 164 |
| vast potential | 155 |
| venal | 106 |
| venality | 106 |
| venerable | 109 |
| verbal intervention | 56 |
| veto | 131 |
| viability | 154 |
| viable business | 154 |
| vibrant | 14 |
| Vice President | 99 |
| vice president | 105 |
| vie with him | 87 |
| village assembly | 128 |
| village hall | 128 |
| violation of the Public Offices Election Law | 85 |
| virtuoso | 166 |
| vital | 14 |
| vocal | 121 |
| void | 92,136 |
| volume | 61 |
| voluntary restraint[rule] | 47 |
| volunteer activities | 41 |
| vote | 91 |
| vote counting | 92 |
| vote (for) | 91 |
| vote rigging | 92 |
| voters | 90 |
| voters' list | 90 |
| voucher | 25 |
| vow | 89 |
| vulnerable | 80 |

## W

| Term | Page |
|---|---|
| wafer-thin victory | 93 |
| wage claim | 36 |
| wage freeze | 36 |
| wait for a high (ball) | 186 |
| walk | 180 |
| walk out | 79 |
| walking papers | 35 |
| wane | 112 |
| warily | 66 |
| wash out the effort | 131 |
| waste pitch | 181 |
| watershed | 119 |
| weak grounder | 188 |
| weak yen | 54 |
| weakling | 160 |
| web of corporate alliances | 49 |
| web site | 153 |
| whiff | 177 |
| wholesale prices | 18 |
| wholesome | 26 |
| wide off the mark | 112 |
| wide-ranging partnership | 39 |
| widening trade surplus | 45 |
| wild pitch | 181 |
| win | 93 |
| win a seat | 93 |
| win against | 169 |
| win by default | 80 |
| win the championship | 81,170 |
| win the pennant | 170 |
| win the tournament | 81 |
| windfall | 29 |
| window dressing (financial records) | 29 |
| wine and dine | 140 |
| winless | 80 |
| winning pitcher | 175 |
| winning streak | 169 |
| winning trick [way] | 79 |
| winningest pitcher | 176 |
| wire-tapping bill | 129 |
| with the stream | 114 |
| withdraw from the tournament | 80 |
| withholding tax | 71 |
| women's suffrage | 84 |
| work the ninth (inning) | 175 |
| World Trade Organization [WTO] | 49 |
| wrap-up | 115 |
| wrestle (with) | 76 |
| (wrestling) bout | 78 |
| write off | 26 |
| wrongdoing | 141 |

## Y

| Term | Page |
|---|---|
| Y2K problem | 153 |
| year on year | 46 |
| yen quotation | 54 |
| yen's appreciation | 54 |
| yen's depreciation | 54 |
| yield | 61,63,182 |
| You put the cart before the horse. | 117 |
| young at heart | 108 |

## Z

| Term | Page |
|---|---|
| zero growth | 17 |
| zero in | 89 |

井上一馬［いのうえ・かずま］

1956年、東京生まれ。比較文学論を学んだ後、アメリカの文化・社会の研究と紹介、作家活動を続けている。
著書に『英語できますか？——究極の学習法』『試行錯誤の文章教室』『アメリカ映画の大教科書（上・下）』『シリコンバレー戦国史』（以上、新潮選書）、『天職をつかんだ9人の女性』（中央公論新社）、『ブロードウェイ・ミュージカル』（文春新書）、『ケネディ——その実像を求めて』『ブラック・ムービー』（以上、講談社現代新書）、『マドンナのアメリカ』『夫婦で子育てしてますか？』（以上、PHP研究所）、訳書にボブ・グリーン著『アメリカン・ビート』（河出文庫）、『十七歳』（文春文庫）など。

話すための英語 ニュース・ビジネス＆スポーツ編（上）

二〇〇〇年三月六日　第一版第一刷
二〇〇〇年九月十二日　第一版第三刷

著者────井上一馬
発行者────江口克彦
発行所────PHP研究所

東京本部　〒102-83331 千代田区三番町3-10
第一出版部　☎03-3239-6221
普及一部　☎03-3239-6233

京都本部　〒601-8411 京都市南区西九条北ノ内町11

制作協力・組版　PHPエディターズ・グループ
装幀者────芦澤泰偉
印刷所・製本所　図書印刷株式会社

©Inoue Kazuma 2000 Printed in Japan
落丁・乱丁本は送料弊社負担にてお取り替えいたします。
ISBN4-569-61011-0

PHP新書 107

## PHP新書刊行にあたって

「繁栄を通じて平和と幸福を」(PEACE and HAPPINESS through PROSPERITY)の願いのもと、PHP研究所が創設されて今年で五十周年を迎えます。その歩みは、日本人が先の戦争を乗り越え、並々ならぬ努力を続けて、今日の繁栄を築き上げてきた軌跡に重なります。

しかし、平和で豊かな生活を手にした現在、多くの日本人は、自分が何のために生きているのか、どのように生きていきたいのかを、見失いつつあるように思われます。そして、その間にも、日本国内や世界のみならず地球規模での大きな変化が日々生起し、解決すべき問題となって私たちのもとに押し寄せてきます。

このような時代に人生の確かな価値を見出し、生きる喜びに満ちあふれた社会を実現するために、いま何が求められているのでしょうか。それは、先達が培ってきた知恵を紡ぎ直すこと、その上で自分たち一人一人がおかれた現実と進むべき未来について丹念に考えていくこと以外にはありません。

その営みは、単なる知識に終わらない深い思索へ、そしてよく生きるための哲学への旅でもあります。所が創設五十周年を迎えましたのを機に、PHP新書を創刊し、この新たな旅を読者と共に歩んでいきたいと思っています。多くの読者の共感と支援を心よりお願いいたします。

一九九六年十月

PHP研究所